METHUEN'S Ⓜ OUTLINES

ANCIENT GREECE

by

DUNCAN TAYLOR

With Illustrations by
KATERINA WILCZYNSKI

METHUEN & CO. LTD.
36 ESSEX STREET · STRAND · LONDON · WC2

First published 1957

To NEIL

ὁ δὲ ἀνεξέταστος βίος οὐ βιωτός . . .

These words from the *Apology of Socrates* mean:
"The unexamined life is unlivable." That is to say,
you should always ask questions, not only of others, but
also of yourself.

———————

The illustrations are by Katerina Wilczynski, except the maps and seven illustrations
(pp. 10, 23, 41, 42) by Clare Brelstaff.

Catalogue No. 5994/U

PRINTED IN GREAT BRITAIN
BY W. & J. MACKAY & CO. LTD., CHATHAM

CONTENTS

Throwing the discus

Modern Greek postage stamps. Left, Zeus casts a thunderbolt

GREECE is a country that people go to on cruises in spring, summer and autumn. Like other people who go on cruises, they are in search of sunshine. They pack bathing suits. But, unlike most other people who go on cruises, they also pack a lot of books—*The Iliad, The Odyssey, How to enjoy Greek Art, The Greek City-State, The Plays of Sophocles.* Some of the books are in Greek, e.g., *'ΑΠΟΛΟΓΙΑ ΣΩΚΡΑΤΟΥΣ—The Apology of Socrates.*

There is another queer thing about cruising to Greece. The labels on the passengers' luggage probably do not have the word "Greece" on them at all. Instead you will find the word "Hellenic". This is a "Hellenic" cruise and the king of the country the passengers are about to visit is called King of the Hellenes, not King of Greece. When they buy their first postage stamps after arriving in Athens they will find them inscribed *ΕΛΛΑΣ*, which in English would be written HELLAS.

The fact is that the Greeks, who call themselves Hellenes for a reason which is explained in the next section, have a very long and in some respects very splendid history. They are proud of it and people of other countries approach Greece with reverence.

Reverence means loving and admiring at the same time. It is a much more serious feeling than usually comes over a person looking at Stonehenge or the Pyramids.

WHO WERE THE HELLENES?

Who were the Hellenes, whom we call Greeks because the Romans called them Greeks? This is the first of many questions about early Greek history to which there are two answers—the truth, as far as we have been able to get at it, and the myths and legends told among the ancient Greeks themselves.

It is usually convenient to put the old story first and the truth, as far as it is

Physical features of Greece

known, second. For the truth is usually shorter and duller.

The Greek story of the creation of the world told how, in the beginning, there was Chaos; then came Gaea, the broad, firm, flat Earth with a dark region called Tartarus below. Gaea produced Uranus (Heaven), the mountains and the sea.

Gaea then married Uranus. Their children, among them the Titans, were fero-

cious and undisciplined. Uranus stuffed them away into cavities in the earth. Gaea did not like this. She produced iron and made a weapon which the Titan Cronus used to dethrone his father.

Cronus was afraid that his children would treat him as roughly as he had treated Uranus. Eventually they did. One of them, Zeus, led the others in a revolt against their father. Cronus and the

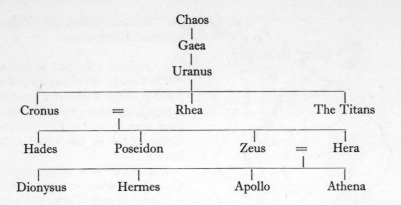

A family tree, showing some of the principal gods and goddesses. Uranus married his mother; Cronus and Zeus married their sisters.

Titans held out in a tremendous struggle which lasted ten years, but they were finally defeated and thrust down into Tartarus.

Thereafter Zeus reigned supreme on Mt Olympus, relying on his two weapons—thunder and lightning. One of his brothers, Poseidon, became lord of the sea. The other, Hades, was made ruler of the underworld, where men dragged out a sombre and shadowy existence after death.

Zeus had many wives, of whom Hera, who was also his sister, was the chief.

He also had many children, among them Apollo (God of prophecy, poetry and music) Dionysus or Bacchus (God of wine) Hermes (Messenger of the Gods) and Athena. Athena's mother was the wisest of the goddesses and Zeus was warned that any children she might bear would grow to be stronger than he. So the story was that Zeus swallowed this wise goddess. Her child, Athena, later sprang fully armed out of the top of his head. She had inherited her mother's brains. So she became the goddess of wisdom, but she was also a warrior goddess, who wore armour and never married.

Zeus had other worries as well as the headache which produced Athena. One of the biggest of these worries was the badness of men. Zeus decided that the best remedy for this was to submerge the whole of Greece with torrential rain. Everyone was drowned except for one man, Deucalion, and his wife Pyrrha. They had been warned in time for them to build an ark which floated over the flood waters and finally beached on Mount Parnassus.

Hermes was then sent to offer Deucalion a gift from Zeus. Deucalion said that what his wife and he wanted most of all was company. They were told to throw stones over their heads. These turned into men and women. Later, however, Deucalion and Pyrrha settled down and brought up a family. One of their sons was Hellen. From him, it was said, the Hellenes were descended.

3

The Minotaur

So much for the myths. In fact, all we know about the Hellenes is that they were a tribe in northern Greece whose name gradually came to be used not only by the whole of mainland Greece but by Greeks everywhere—in Asia Minor, on the islands and in colonies all round the Mediterranean.

As you will see, the Greeks fought each other frequently and never united for long. But they felt that they all had something in common compared with non-Greeks, whom they called *barbarians*.

So "Hellas" meant the whole of the scattered Greek world.

THESEUS AND THE MINOTAUR

The Greeks, then, had their story of the creation of the world, of a great flood and a heroic ancestor; but the only *fact* we have met so far is that a tribe called Hellenes did in fact exist in Northern Greece.

The search now turns southward, to Crete. Once again we begin with a legend.

Minos, King of Crete, had a brilliantly athletic son, Androgeus, a beautiful daughter, Ariadne, and a monster, the Minotaur, (half bull, half man).

The Minotaur was kept shut up in a *labyrinth*, a vast network of caves and underground passages, designed by Daedalus, a brilliant Athenian exile.

Androgeus was happy and successful. Too successful. For, when he had competed in the games at Athens and won every event, Aegeus, King of Athens, had him put to death. Minos then made war on the Athenians to avenge his son's death, and compelled them to send seven youths and seven maidens to Crete every year as victims for the Minotaur.

When he grew up, Theseus, the son of King Aegeus, volunteered to be one of the unlucky fourteen, and sailed with them to Crete in their black-sailed ship. He had made up his mind to kill the Minotaur. King Aegeus, praying that his son might succeed, had a white sail put on board the ship and gave orders for it to be hoisted on the homeward voyage, if Theseus were alive.

In Crete, Ariadne the daughter of King Minos, helped Theseus by giving him a ball of thread. He fixed the end of this at the entrance of the labyrinth and unwound it as he went along. So he not only succeeded in killing the Minotaur but was also able to escape with his companions.

On the voyage back to Athens there was a good deal of excitement. Nobody remembered to hoist the white sail. Old Aegeus, who was watching for it, saw the black one, and thinking Theseus was dead, threw himself into the sea, since when it has been called the Aegean after him.

THE PALACE OF MINOS

So much for the legend. What of the facts?

At Cnossos, near Herakleion, in Crete are the ruins of an enormous palace, which must have needed somebody like Daedalus to design it.

Its honeycomb of cavernous cellars, traces of which still remain, might well have given rise to stories of a "labyrinth", and though no pictures of the Minotaur himself have been found, bulls occur frequently in the paintings which can still be seen upon the palace walls.

Sir Arthur Evans began to excavate this great palace in 1899 and called it "The Palace of Minos". He did not find evidence that a king called Minos had built it. Minos remains legendary. But the name was dignified and convenient.

From excavations at Cnossos and elsewhere in Crete, it has been possible to trace the history of Cretan civilization back to about 3000 B.C. So it is here, not on the mainland, that a history of Greece ought to begin.

Crete is only 180 miles from the coast of

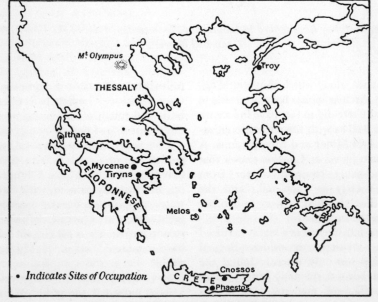

Centres of Early Aegean Civilisation

5

Mycenae, as it may have looked in the time of Agamemnon. Part of the Lion Gate (right) can still be seen.

North Africa, along which ships could sail to Egypt. Archaeologists have been able to show that Crete did in fact have links with Egypt as well as with the ancient civilizations of Asia Minor and Mesopotamia. A copper axe found at Cnossos shows that Crete probably received copper from Egypt as early as 3000 B.C., and the Cretans later learned pottery and other arts from the Egyptians.

By 2000 B.C. Crete was a highly civilized country. Writing, to which dogged scholarship has only recently found the key, had been developed; but as there were no papyrus marshes, clay tablets were used. The pottery and metalwork industries had made a thriving foreign trade possible. The first palaces had been built and much of the island was united under one line of Kings.

The years 1600 to 1400 B.C. were the golden age of Crete. It is to this period that the Palace of Minos belongs. It was big and brightly painted, with an efficient water supply and drainage system. The great town of Cnossos, of which this palace formed the most elegant part, may have contained about eighty thousand people (i.e. it was comparable in size to Exeter, Cambridge or Motherwell).

After 1400 B.C. the power of Crete declined and by about 1200 supremacy in the

Aegean had shifted to the mainland—not to Athens, but to the cities of Mycenae and Tiryns in the Peloponnese. Their inhabitants, the Achaeans, had learned from the Cretans to make fine pottery and metalwork and to put up big stone buildings, but they also surrounded their cities with massive walls, which the Cretans had never built, since they relied upon their fleet for defence.

The Achaeans of this time, however, are remembered in history as besiegers rather than besieged. It was they who fought against Troy. Once again, where legend is mixed with fact, it will be best to begin with the legend.

HELEN OF TROY

Helen "of Troy" was in fact Helen of Sparta where she was the wife of King Menelaus. She only spent part of her life in Troy, but it was those years which made her famous. The cause of her going there was the following.

The three goddesses, Hera, Athena, and Aphrodite (goddess of love) were attending a wedding, when a golden apple was thrown among the guests. It was inscribed "to the fairest". Naturally, each of the three goddesses claimed it. Zeus ordered Hermes to take them to Mount Ida, near Troy, where Paris would settle their dispute. Paris was the son of King Priam, but it had been prophesied that he would cause trouble; so he had left the court and was working on Mount Ida as a shepherd.

Instead of letting Paris decide simply by looking at them, the three goddesses all offered him bribes. Hera said she would make him a powerful ruler if he chose her. Athena offered him fame as a warrior. But Aphrodite promised Paris that if he would award her the golden apple she would give him the most beautiful woman in the world for his wife.

Paris gave the golden apple to Aphrodite.

Aphrodite kept her promise, but not in the way one might have expected. Instead of finding a beautiful unmarried girl for Paris, she caused him to fall in love with Helen of Sparta and he eloped with her to Troy. This was an outrageous thing to do. It is not surprising that the poets who told the story made Helen of Troy the cause of a ten year war.

THE WOODEN HORSE

In the tenth year of the war the Greek hero Achilles slew Hector, the Trojan, in single combat. (Paris, the cause of all the trouble, never distinguished himself very much in the fighting.) The death of Hector was a cruel blow to the Trojans, particularly to Hector's old father Priam; but they still did not surrender. In the end they were beaten by a trick.

The Greeks built a huge wooden horse, big enough to hold a number of fully armed men. They put the pick of their warriors inside the horse and left it on the shore. All the rest of the Greek army sailed away. The Trojans were supposed to think that the Greeks had given up hope and gone home; but in fact they had only withdrawn to an island nearby.

The Trojans streamed out of their city and strolled delightedly through the deserted Greek camp and along the shore where the Greek ships had been drawn up. But the wooden horse started them arguing. Should they destroy it? Or should they drag it into their city and keep it there as a memorial of their victory?

One Trojan, Laocöon, had no doubts. "I fear the Greeks, even when they bring us gifts", he said, and threw his spear at the horse's great wooden belly. There was a hollow sound and perhaps Laocöon would have persuaded the Trojans to open up the horse straight away if their attention had not at that moment been distracted by something even more interesting—the discovery of a live Greek.

This Greek was a young spy named Sinon. His hands were bound and he had a plausible story to tell. The Greeks, he said, had been going to make a human sacrifice of him in order to ensure that the gods would grant them a calm voyage home; everything was ready; but he had managed to escape just in time and since then had been in hiding, with his hands still firmly bound.

The soft-hearted Trojans swallowed this story whole. Sinon was set free. Everyone was kind to him. And of course they asked his advice about the wooden horse; which was just what Sinon and the Greek generals had intended.

Sinon was a good actor. Now was his big scene. He put on a very worried expression, as though it grieved him to betray the secrets of the Greeks even though they had treated him so badly. The Trojans waited while he said how it hurt him to betray his countrymen, how he hated having to do it, how he never would have done it if they had not treated him so cruelly.

The Trojans were still waiting for advice about the horse. At last Sinon told them the "secret". It was this.

The Greeks had been told by their priest that to ensure a safe voyage home they should make a great offering to Athena, the Goddess who had helped them throughout the war. But the offering would have to be one which could not be stolen by the Trojans. Hence the wooden horse. "Make it immense", the priest had said, "so that our enemies cannot take it into Troy. For, if they do, we are doomed. But if the Trojans tamper with the horse where it stands, *they* are doomed."

Sinon's advice was exactly the opposite of Laocöon's. Unfortunately there was no time for discussion, because at that moment two enormous sea serpents plunged ashore, twined themselves round Laocöon and his two little sons, and crushed them to pulp. The Trojans concluded that the gods were angry with Laocöon for throwing his spear at the horse. Obviously, they thought, Sinon was right. They must bring the horse into the city. So they tore down part of the walls, fitted wheels to the horse and dragged it in.

During the night, of course, the Greeks landed again. At a given signal Sinon opened the horse and warriors swarmed out. They caused panic in the city and were easily able to open the gates for their comrades who had now gathered outside the walls.

Thus, after ten years, Troy fell.

WAS THERE A TROJAN WAR?

Parts of the story of the Trojan War are told in two poems the *Iliad* (Ilium= Troy) and the *Odyssey* (Odysseus was one of the Greek Generals) by Homer, the earliest Greek poet. A hundred years ago the war was regarded as a legend, but a German-American, Heinrich Schliemann, who had learned to love Homer as a boy and became immensely rich, determined to try and find Troy by digging. He succeeded, in 1871, and later proceeded to excavate Mycenae. He made many mistakes, but his work and the work of those who followed him have made it possible to answer 'Yes' to the question 'Was there a Trojan War?'

We now know that from about 2500 B.C. a number of great cities existed on the site of Troy, each one built on top of the ruins of its predecessor.

The sixth city was built about 1500 B.C. and its destruction by the Greeks is now thought to have taken place about 1180 B.C., that is, about the time when the great days of Mycenae were coming to an end.

We know nothing at all about the course of the war, but its cause may well have been a quarrel over Black Sea trade.

Troy's position naturally tempted her to try and exact tribute from ships passing through the Hellespont.

Homer and the archaeologists thus give us some sort of picture of the Greeks in about 1200 B.C. But after the end of the Trojan War we enter a period of several centuries about which neither legends nor written accounts nor archaeologists can tell us very much.

ON THE MOVE

The "Dark Age" of Greece (c. 1100–800) was a time of migration and settlement. Whole peoples were on the move. People on the move do not have time to write records for us to read later nor do they build palaces which we can dig up. So there is no continuous history of this period, though during it Homer (c. 900) and Hesiod (c. 800) wrote their poems.

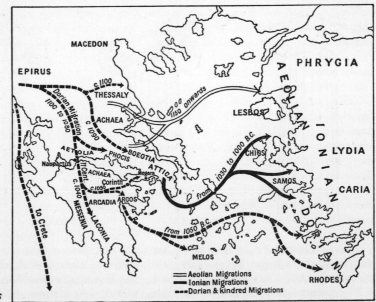

Early Migrations

9

(Hesiod's contained two very different ingredients—stories of the gods and practical advice about country life.)

The Achaeans were overcome by invaders from the north called Dorians, who occupied the Peloponnese. Some of them also occupied part of the coast of Asia Minor and Crete. The Dorians did not invade the peninsula on which Athens stood, but Achaeans and kindred peoples called Ionians, who had been forced out of other parts of Greece, took refuge there. In time some of these migrated to Asia Minor. The coastal area which they occupied was called Ionia.

The distinction between Dorian and non-Dorian parts of Greece gradually ceased to be important. The point to remember about the Dorian invasion is that it left Greeks settled in Ionia as well as on the Aegean islands and the mainland. They were destined, however, to go further afield than that.

CITY-STATES AND COLONIES

The two hundred years after 800 B.C. saw a great expansion of the Greeks by colonisation. Colonisation is a more orderly kind of migration. The Greeks now lived in numerous small communities, often no more than towns with surrounding farmlands. They are therefore called "city-states". Some of these city-states now sent out colonies to southern Italy, Sicily and also to the Black Sea. These colonies became independent but they kept in touch with their mother-city. Miletus in Ionia sent out many of the Black Sea colonies. Byzantium, now Istanbul, was founded by Megara, a city near Athens. The most important of the western colonies, Syra-

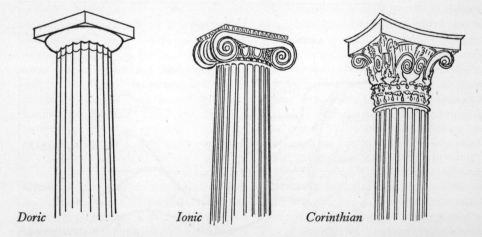

Doric   Ionic   Corinthian

The names Doric and Ionic have been given to the two simplest types of capital (the top of an architectural column); but this does not mean that one sort was used only by Dorians and the other by Ionians (e.g. the Parthenon has Doric capitals). Similarly, the Corinthian capital, introduced in the fourth century B.C., was not confined to Corinth.

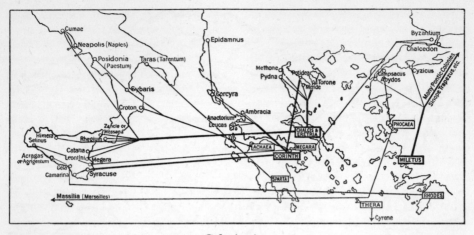

Colonisation

cuse, was founded by Corinth. Sparta founded Taras (Taranto) in Italy. Marseilles in the south of France was first colonised by Greeks from Asia Minor. One of the Aegean islands founded Cyrene in North Africa. A map of the Greek world about 600 B.C., when the period of colonisation was over, has therefore to cover most of the Mediterranean.

When a people expands in this way it is usual to speak of their "empire" and a map of it shows somewhere a city in extra large print, which is the capital—Babylon, for example, or Egyptian Thebes, or Rome. At this time (c. 600 B.C.) the Greek city-states and their colonies, being independent of each other, did not constitute an empire and acknowledged no capital. There were however two places which all Greeks regarded with reverence. One was Delphi and the other was Olympia.

THE DELPHIC ORACLE

The Delphic oracle, the priestess of Apollo, was supposed to have the gift of prophecy. She was consulted before a colony was founded, before war was declared and on all sorts of other questions.

When a request for advice was put to her through her priests she proceeded to put herself into a trance. She is said to have done this by chewing laurel leaves, drinking water from an underground stream and inhaling an evil-smelling gas which arose through a cleft in the rocks within her shrine (but no traces of this cleft have been found). Finally, seated on a tripod, she spoke. The priests claimed to be able to make sense of her utterances. After listening, they presented a reply, in verse, to the questioner.

The priests acquired great power, but if they had abused it grossly, Delphi would not have maintained its importance for centuries, as it did. Replies to political questions obviously had to be ambiguous, but when consulted on private affairs the oracle tended to be on the side of what we would now consider right (e.g. in favour of mercy and against fraud). It

View from Delphi. The hillsides are rough and studded with olive trees. In the distance lies the Corinthian Gulf and, beyond it, the Peloponnese. (Inset) The kind of tripod on which the priestess is said to have sat while receiving inspiration from Apollo.

was not, however, the formal reply alone which made a visit to Delphi worth while. As at international conferences nowadays, all sorts of informal meetings and conversations must have taken place. Nowhere else could one find out so much about the scattered communities of the Greek world.

THE OLYMPIC GAMES

At Olympia every four years games were held in which any Greek was entitled to take part. It is not known when the first games were held, but they were said to have been revived in the year 776 B.C. and the Greeks used that year from which to reckon dates. The period of four years between each celebration of the games was called an *Olympiad*. When therefore a Greek writer says something happened in the year of the . . . Olympiad we can calculate the year according to our system and put it down as . . . B.C. From now onwards Greek history becomes more exact.

Like Delphi, Olympia became a place where men from any part of the Greek world might meet. For a month every four years the incessant quarrels of the city-states were stopped, and during five days of this truce period the games were held. There was running, long jump, boxing, wrestling, throwing the discus or javelin, chariot racing and horse racing (all

Wrestlers. Athletes wore no clothes. These two have rubbed themselves with oil and with fine sand, to give a better grip. Their long hair has been plaited and the plaits are arranged round their heads, giving the effect of a cap.

individual events—no team games). And no Marathon (see p. 29). The only prize at Olympia was a crown of wild olive, but when victorious competitors reached home they were given a variety of honours and rewards. At Athens they received a large sum of money and the right to free dinners for life (cf. p. 60). At Sparta they were assigned the post of honour in battle.

SPARTA

This striking difference in the way Athens and Sparta treated their victorious athletes reflects a striking difference between the states themselves. Neither was important as a coloniser. But during the 6th and 5th centuries they occupy the centre of the stage.

At Sparta living was hard; hence the adjective "Spartan". In the Mycenaean Age, when, according to legend, Menelaus was King of Sparta and Helen was his queen, the place had not yet gained this reputation for hardness, which was a result of the Dorian invasion.

The invaders found the valley of Lacedaemon attractive. They settled there and made the district round Sparta the centre from which they governed. But they did not mix with the previous inhabitants of the country. They enslaved them. These slaves, called *Helots*, were much more numerous than the Spartans themselves.

As a result of two wars (c. 736 and 650 B.C.) against the pre-Dorian inhabitants of Messenia, the Spartans reduced them also to Helot status. But in spite of their military strength the Spartans were at this time still a cultured people, honoured for their poets and musicians, and it was to one of their wise men, Chilon, that the celebrated Greek maxims "Know thyself" and "Nothing in excess" were ascribed. Their craftsmen produced fine pottery and ivory carvings.

It was probably not till after the second Messenian war that the Spartans, in order to keep control of their greatly increased Helot population, began that system of cheerless, iron discipline which made them famous. Tradition attributed its introduction to a certain Lycurgus.

How much Lycurgus had to do with the moulding of the Spartan system, or whether he ever existed at all, we do not know. It is the system itself which is important, because it did not change very much throughout the next three centuries and made Sparta the leading military power in Greece.

Two Kings headed the Spartan state, but they were not all-powerful. Laws were passed and important decisions taken by a Council of twenty-eight citizens, all over sixty years of age, who held office for life. There was also a popular Assembly ("popular" in this sense means "of the people") but it never gained the degree of power enjoyed by the popular Assembly of Athens, of which much will be heard later. There is no doubt that of the three partners in Spartan government—Kings, Council and Assembly—the Council were the most important; though in time of war the Kings came into their own. It was they who commanded the Spartan armies and each had his personal bodyguard of three hundred picked men.

After a time, however, the power of the Kings in war and of the Council of old men in peace received a check. The popular assembly was given the right to elect five officials called *Ephors* every year. These Ephors were able to take part in the discussions of the Council and to make it do what they wanted. In war they could accompany the Kings on their campaigns and a King who disagreed with an Ephor could find himself put on trial when he returned home.

It is astonishing, in view of the great power that the Ephors came to enjoy, that none of them tried, either alone or with a group of his colleagues, to set up a dictatorship. That they did not is another tribute to Spartan discipline.

A SPARTAN GROWS UP

A Spartan child was examined at birth. A healthy infant was allowed to live. Weaklings were not wanted. They were left in the mountains to die. (Exposure of unwanted children was not peculiar to Sparta. Even civilized 5th-century Athenians practised it.)

At the age of seven a Spartan boy left home. His period of family life was finished. Thereafter he would be a member of a community. In modern terms, he would always be either at a boarding school or on military service.

In the "pack", as it was called, the seven-year-old newcomer quickly learned obedience. He had to act as a kind of servant to one of the older boys. He learned to be hardy, since even in winter he had to go barefoot and was only allowed a single garment. He learned to use initiative and was even encouraged to steal in order to increase his rations, which were purposely kept small. It was one of these thieving raids which gave rise to the story of the Spartan boy and the fox. The boy had stolen a fox, and hid it under his cloak. It began to gnaw at his stomach, but to set it free would have meant discovery. The boy therefore let it go on gnawing and at last fell down dead, but with his honour preserved.

Education at Athens was less brutal than at Sparta. An Athenian boy practised athletics, but he also learned music and poetry. Here a boy is being heard a piece of poetry he has learned—probably Homer, whose works had to be known thoroughly. Written exercises were done on wooden tablets covered with wax. A pointed metal instrument was used. The man on the right is a slave, though you could not tell this from his dress. He escorts the boy to and from the lesson. Like other older men he is bearded and carries a long walking-stick. All three of the group have fairly long hair, kept in place by a band, but not as elegantly plaited as the wrestlers' (page 13) or the banqueter's (page 63).

The incidentals of this story are puzzling. If the fox was stolen, it must presumably have belonged to someone. Was it a pet? It seems an odd animal to steal if you are hungry. However, there is no doubt about the moral. Death to a Spartan, even in boyhood, was preferable to the taint of cowardice.

The education of girls was milder; but compared with the education of Athenian girls it was tough and unrestricted. At Athens athletics were a monopoly of the male; but a Spartan girl was encouraged to take part in sports such as running, throwing the javelin and even wrestling, while men and boys looked on.

When he was grown-up a Spartan continued to live in barracks, as a member of a sort of "officers' mess", though he might sleep at home after he was thirty. He had to contribute a fixed amount of barley meal, wine, cheese, dried figs and meat to

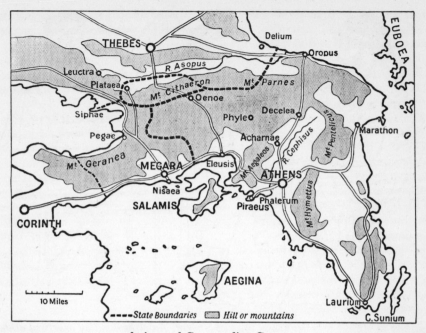

Attica and Surrounding Country

the mess every month. He might marry, but he saw very little of his wife. Soldiering was his life. He had always to be ready for a battle with the Helots. There was a special corps of secret police, whose duty it was to seek out any Helot who seemed to be a trouble-maker and kill him.

The constant danger of attack by the people they had enslaved made the Spartan system work. As we have seen, the Ephors did not attempt dictatorship, and anyone who might have thought of getting a special position for himself by means of wealth was prevented in two ways. Firstly, no Spartan might engage in commerce. Secondly there was no gold or silver coinage—only bars of iron. Lycurgus, or whoever made this last provision, knew

well that a fortune in gold might be hidden under the floor, but a fortune in iron bars would need to be reckoned by the cartload. Concealment would be impossible.

It is not surprising that the superb military machine which the Spartans developed was effective against their neighbours as well as against the Helots. In 546 B.C. Argos, once the leading city of the Peloponnese, was defeated and by about the year 500 almost every city in the peninsula, and Megara outside it, had joined an alliance which acknowledged Sparta as its head.

Not many miles beyond Megara, if one was travelling from the Peloponnese, lay Athens. But there was no question of

Athens joining the Spartan alliance. Her development in the centuries before 500 B.C. had been very different.

ATHENS

The legend of Theseus and the Minotaur suggests that Athens had dealings with Crete during the Minoan and Mycenaean Ages. We have no written history of that time, though the discoveries of archaeologists show that the Acropolis, a rocky mass 512 feet high, already had fortifications like those found at Tiryns and Mycenae.

At the time of the first Olympiad (776 B.C.) there may still have been a King upon the throne, but at Athens, as in many other Greek states, government by Kings gave way about that time to government by the nobles. Monarchy, that is to say, gave way to *aristocracy*. Sparta with her two Kings was an exception.

Whoever ruled Athens also ruled Attica. This was not a district of great natural riches. As can be seen from the map, much of it was mountainous and the corn grown on the plains was not enough when the population increased. However, olives and vines were plentiful and the mountains, as well as providing a home for goats and bees, contained silver and lead mines and marble quarries. In the river beds lay a reddish clay suitable for pottery. Finally, there were good harbours.

Attica, therefore, though not rich, had considerable natural advantages and we shall see how well she used them—how the red clay was turned into pots and the marble into temples, while the harbours were crowded with merchantmen and ships of war. But the most famous product of Attica was neither animal, vegetable nor mineral. It was the form of government known as democracy.

We have now to see how democracy grew out of the aristocracy, or rule of nobles, which succeeded the period of the Kings.

The Spartans had tried to prevent one man becoming much richer than another by using iron bars as money (p. 16). In this rejection of a coinage system they were exceptional. Other Greek states had begun to use silver coins, which seem to have originated in Lydia, a kingdom in Asia Minor, not long after the year 700. It was obviously useful, at that time of colonisation and expanding trade, to be able to avoid the primitive system of barter and sell goods for coins which could

Athenian drachma. Athena's head on one side; the owl and the olive, sacred to her, on the other. An obol ($\frac{1}{6}$ of a drachma) was similar, only smaller. The drachma was the usual daily wage of those who were paid by the day. There were no variations according to skill. Architect and labourer received the same. But there was also piece-work, e.g. 60 drachmas for a full-size marble statue, 20 for a statue of a child. An agricultural labourer got 4 obols a day and his food. A single man could live comfortably on 120 drachma a year. There were 60 unpaid holidays in the year, but of course there were no Sundays.

17

be easily stored, rather than for other goods, which might have to be kept in a warehouse, until it was convenient to exchange them for something else. (See Quiggin, *The Story of Money*.)

So wealth accumulated, but not in everybody's purse. The wealthy, if they were shrewd, became wealthier; the poor got into debt, found themselves unable to pay and were reduced to serfdom, performing compulsory service on the land, or were sold into slavery. This was possible because, under the aristocratic system of government, the poorer people had very little power.

At the head of the government were the *archons*, officials who were elected annually. But no poor man could be archon nor could he take part in making laws. In fact the bulk of the people did not know what the laws were. It was considered a great advance when, in 621 B.C., an archon called Draco had them written down.

The laws of Draco were ferocious. As in Britain, during the early nineteenth century, the death penalty was imposed for quite small thefts. The word "Draconian" has passed into the English language and is applied to any system of laws which is harsh and brutal. But, though the laws themselves were hard, the fact of having them written down gave the oppressed more chance of being dealt with justly.

SOLON

One of the young Athenians who must have taken a good deal of interest in Draco's writing down of the laws was Solon. He came of a good family. His father had been extravagant and this had prompted Solon to become a foreign trader in order to repair the family fortunes. But there was no question of his considering himself one of the oppressed. He was a "have" not a "have-not". Yet Solon was destined to repeal almost all of Draco's laws and to set Athens on the road to democracy.

We first meet Solon as a poet, patriot and soldier. The possession of the island of Salamis was in dispute between Megara and Athens. Athens, to Solon's disgust, renounced her claim. Solon rushed into the market place and recited a poem in which he appealed to the Athenians to reverse their decision and conquer the island. The poem had the desired effect. Solon was chosen to lead the attack and eventually Salamis became part of Attica. A little over a century later the decisive sea-battle of the Persian wars was fought in the stretch of water which separated Salamis from the mainland.

Meanwhile discontent due to poverty and debt had reached such a pitch that the

Olives and twig

An olive tree. Its foliage is not thick and the bright light on its silvery leaves makes them look transparent. These trees, which look so bare, were (and still are) of great value to the Greeks. An olive twig curls naturally when you pick it, so that two twigs easily make a victor's crown. The leaves are greyish green on one side and silvery on the other.

After 16 years the trees begin to bear olives, coloured greyish green, the size of a damson. They are eaten with bread or crushed to make oil which is used for cooking. The ancient Greeks also used olive oil in lamps and for rubbing on their bodies (they had no soap). As well as being indispensable at home, the oil provided a valuable export.

need for firm action was clear. Solon was liked and trusted. When he was elected archon in 594 B.C. he was able to begin a programme of reform.

Solon's first act was to free all those who had enslaved themselves on account of debt and make it illegal for any citizen to do so again in the future. Other measures were aimed at checking extravagance. For instance, not more than a certain sum might be spent on funerals or on the dowry of a bride. Last of what may be called Solon's restrictive measures was the prohibition of the export of corn. There was not sufficient for home consumption but merchants had been exporting because they found it more profitable. Henceforth only olive oil might be exported.

Solon's constructive measures were intended to encourage manufactures. Every father was compelled to teach his sons a trade and foreign craftsmen were encouraged to settle at Athens (though they did not become full citizens). Corinthian pottery was already famous. Vases, bowls and jugs made from the reddish Attic clay and decorated with black figures now began to rival the Corinthian ware. Incidentally, this black-figured pottery and the red-figured pottery which succeeded it in the 5th century B.C. is one of our best sources for finding out what Athenians wore and how they lived. Many of the drawings in this book are based on black- or red-figured pottery, but the figures cannot be copied exactly because in the original they were on a curved surface.

Having freed the poor of debt and laid the foundations of industrial prosperity Solon arranged that the privileges and responsibilities of government should be more equally shared. Even the poorest citizens were to be members of a People's Assembly and they might also serve as jurors in a People's Law Court. This does not mean that Solon led a revolution which overturned the aristocracy. He was, after all, an aristocrat himself and he left the aristocrats still powerful. But when democracy developed fully at Athens during the 5th century Solon was regarded as its founder.

It is said that, having made his laws, Solon left Athens for ten years to give the city a chance to test them. He travelled widely, visiting Egypt, Cyprus and Lydia. The story of his meeting with King Croesus of Lydia cannot be quite true, because Croesus did not become king until 560 B.C., but it is a story which should be known.

Croesus made a great display of his wealth when Solon visited him. Solon, however, was not impressed. Croesus then had him conducted round the royal treasuries, but Solon still did not burst forth into the expressions of amazement and congratulation which were expected of him. Croesus then said, "Tell me, Solon, have you ever known a happier man than I?" "Oh, yes" answered Solon,

Gold coin of Croesus, whose people, the Lydians, are said to have been the first to use coins. But Croesus could not buy happiness.

and proceeded to describe an Athenian, father of a family, honest and fairly well off, who had died fighting for his country. "Anyone else?" asked Croesus, whereupon Solon described two Athenian youths who had died on the same night after dutifully helping their mother the previous day. When Croesus became angry at finding no place for himself in Solon's list of happy men, Solon explained that the Greeks did not believe in congratulating a man on his good fortune, because they knew that later there might be a change for the worse. "We only call a man happy" he added, "if he has gone on being happy until his death. You might say that we look on life as a wrestling match. We do not believe in awarding a crown of victory while the contestants are still grappling with one another. We wait till the end."

Like many people who are given good advice, Croesus did not like it very much at the time. Some years later however his kingdom of Lydia was overthrown by Cyrus the Persian and Croesus found himself bound upon a pyre, about to be burned to death. Solon's words came back to him. "We wait till the end". He saw the point of it now. "O Solon! Solon!" he cried. Cyrus heard him. Was this some God, he asked, this Solon on whom Croesus was calling? Croesus was unbound and brought before his conqueror. When he heard the story, Cyrus was so moved that he cancelled the death sentence and Croesus became one of his firmest friends.

When old Solon came back to Athens after his travels he found people far from contented. There was bitter party strife, and not long after his return the city which Solon had set on the road towards democracy found herself under the rule of a tyrant.

The word *tyrant* in Greek history has a special meaning. Many of the city states passed through a period of *tyranny*, which meant rule by one man, instead of rule by members of the wealthiest families. This one-man rule was often less cruel than rule by the wealthy.

The tyrant looked after the interests of the poor in order to win their support. But not all tyrants were wise and humane. One of them, Phaleris of Acragas in Sicily (c. 560), made a name for himself by burning his enemies in a brazen bull. It is because of that kind of action that the word "tyrant" in English is now only applied to ruthless rulers.

Peisistratus, who now seized power at Athens, was one of the humaner sort of tyrants. He treated Solon as a distinguished elder statesman and Solon, now nearly eighty, does not seem to have protested against the new regime. He did not see very much of it, for in 559 he died. Did he die happy, according to his own standard? Had he been wise in leaving Athens, instead of staying to see that his new laws were kept? Perhaps not. On the other hand if his principle "Wait till the end" is carried a step further, and you take it to mean "Wait for the judgment of history", Solon is happy indeed.

A TYRANT WHO WAS NOT TYRANNICAL

A tyrant's first problem was to seize power. Peisistratus had to solve this problem three times. In 560 he came before a meeting of the Assembly wounded and bleeding, alleging that his political opponents had attacked him. Sympathisers voted him a body-guard, with the aid of which he was able to seize power, but his opponents soon forced him to take flight. His next descent on the city was made in a chariot, in which he was accompanied by a handsome woman dressed up as Athena. He alleged that his companion was in fact Athena and that she had chosen him to rule her city. No doubt this escapade, if it really took place, impressed the simpler supporters of Peisistratus and amused the wiser ones. Anyway he again established himself as tyrant and after another short spell of power was again thrown out.

This time he stayed away ten years. When he returned for the third time, in 546, he made a less spectacular entry than on previous occasions, but remained to rule until his death in 527. During that period his talent for display found a more useful outlet. He organised the annual spring festival of Dionysus, at which the great tragic dramas of the following century were performed, and the Panathenaea, a festival in honour of Athena, which included the recitation of poetry as well as athletics and drew competitors from all over Greece. He saw to it that Athens had buildings and sculpture worthy of her guests.

We have become so accustomed to thinking of Athens as the most splendid city in Greece that it is hard to realise how insignificant she was before about the year 600. Solon having prepared the way, Peisistratus put Athens on the map, not only by skilful showmanship but also by looking ahead. He sent Athenians to establish themselves in Thrace, where he had silver mines, and beside the Hellespont, where they would be able to ensure the safe passage of corn ships from the Black Sea. (Athens could not live without imported corn.) Nor was farming at home forgotten. The land of exiled nobles was divided among landless citizens and money was lent to help them make a start —not on corn growing, however, but on the cultivation of the much more profitable olive tree.

Tyranny at Athens continued to be mild and beneficial even after the death of Peisistratus. His two sons, Hippias and Hipparchus, succeeded him and, surprisingly, did not quarrel. Two nobles, however, Harmodius and Aristogeiton, quarrelled with the tyrant brothers and decided to murder them (514). They made the attempt during the Panathenaea festival, since that was one of the few times when they could carry arms without exciting suspicion. (This shows how peaceful life at Athens had become.) Hipparchus was killed, but Hippias escaped. Of the two murderers, Harmodius was cut down by the guards on the spot and Aristogeiton died later under torture. Hippias now ruled alone, but at this point we can speak of him as a tyrant in the modern sense. He was very frightened and therefore very cruel. With the help of the Spartans the Athenians deposed him. He took refuge with Darius, King of Persia and we shall hear of him again (p. 29).

Why should the Spartans with their harsh, strict form of government, have been interested in freeing Athens from a tyrant? The answer is that the Spartans did not like tyrants. Tyrants were ambitious, which meant that they might build up their city-states into powerful rivals of Sparta. Tyrants often sided with the poor against the rich, whereas the whole

(i)

(iii)

(iv)

(ii)

Greek Pottery. *After rubbing himself with oil from this bottle (i) an athlete might win this vase (ii) at the Panathenaic games. Celebrating his victory he would drink from a cup like this (iii), filled with wine served in a jar like this (iv). These are only a few of the uses of Greek pottery. An unwanted baby was left outside in a jar to die. A dead man's ashes, after cremation, were put in a jar and pottery containing provisions was placed on his grave. Olive oil was exported, and the tribute paid to Athens was stored, in large pottery vessels.*

The best Greek vases are interesting as well as beautiful because they are decorated with pictures of Greek life and legend. (See illustrations pp. 15 and 48.)

Attic potters used a reddish clay. In the 6th century B.C. they painted black figures on it (ii). Later they blackened the vase leaving the figures and ornamentation red (i).

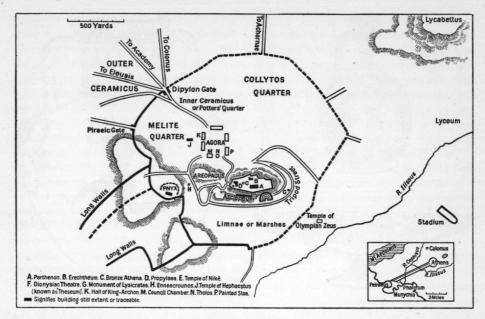

Ancient Athens

A. Parthenon. B. Erechtheum. C. Bronze Athena. D. Propylaea. E. Temple of Nikê.
F. Dionysiac Theatre. G. Monument of Lysicrates. H. Enneacrounos. J. Temple of Hephaestus
(known as Theseum). K. Hall of King-Archon. M. Council Chamber. N. Tholos. P. Painted Stoa.
■ Signifies building still extant or traceable.

Spartan system was aimed at keeping the poor Helots down. Sparta therefore preferred her neighbours to have governments similar to her own aristocracy. She hoped that Hippias would be replaced by a group of nobles who would put the clock back a hundred years and rule Athens again as she had been ruled before the time of Solon. But this was not what happened. On the contrary, in the year 508, under the leadership of a noble called Cleisthenes, Athens was transformed into the democracy which was to astonish the world, and in the process Harmodius and Aristogeiton were transformed in people's minds from a pair of bloodthirsty, squabbling nobles into two unselfish heroes who had shed their blood for freedom.

DEMOCRACY

The heroism of Harmodius and Aristogeiton was a myth, but Athenian democracy was not. In the two great wars of the fifth century—the Persian and the Peloponnesian—the Athenians clearly felt they had what would now be called a "way of life" which was worth fighting for. Cleisthenes, although he was of nobler blood than Solon, gave more power to the poor than Solon had done. Nearly all Athenian citizens now had a vote in the Assembly, a body which approved laws discussed in the Council of Five Hundred. The Five Hundred were elected by the citizens and anyone over thirty could be a member.

As well as taking his share in law-making and government a citizen also played his part as a juryman in seeing that justice was done. Even the archons could be brought to trial when their year of office was over, if they were thought to have misused their power. There was a kind of police force consisting of Scythian archers which Peisistratus had set up. But they were the citizens' servants, not his masters.

There is often a good deal of argument about what is meant by a "free" country. A useful test is to ask: Can police knock on the door in the middle of the night and take people away to death or imprisonment without a public trial? If this "knock on the door" question is asked about fifth-century Athens the answer to it would be: No. There were no secret police and there were no mysterious disappearances in the middle of the night.

These privileges of citizenship, however, were not shared by everyone living in Attica. "An Athenian citizen" does not mean the same as "a resident in Athens".

Neither women nor slaves might vote and immigrants from other cities, *metics*, even though they might be Greeks, found citizens' rights very difficult to obtain, however wealthy they might be. This is one of the two main differences between Athenian and modern democracy. The other is that Athenian citizens attended their Assembly in person. There was no representative government.

Finally, among all the privileges of citizenship, Cleisthenes introduced a new safety measure, *ostracism*. Once a year the Assembly might decide to take a vote on the question whether one of their number should be banished. The method of voting was to write the name of the person you wanted banished on a piece of broken pottery, the Greek word for which is "ostrakon". If at least six thousand votes were cast, the man against whom the majority voted had to go into banishment for ten years. The idea was to prevent a recurrence of tyranny or civil strife. It is said that one of the earliest victims of this ingenious procedure was Cleisthenes.

Unfortunately we do not know for certain how the great law-maker met his end; but as the curtain rises on the fifth century he is no longer on the stage. The year is 498 and the scene shifts from Athens to Asia Minor, whither Athens had sent a small force to help the Ionian Greeks, who had revolted against Persia. This force lit two fires. One was at Sardis; it burned the city to the ground and flickered out. The other was in the heart of Darius, the Persian king; this was a fire of fury that burned on and on. Darius had taken care that it should not go out. Every

Ostracon—a piece of broken pottery used by a voter who wished Aristides to be 'ostracized'. Broken pottery was used as we use scrap paper. This piece has been further chipped since it was written on. Originally it bore the full names of Aristides and his father Lysimachus. (Greeks had no surnames, so they had to be distinguished by adding the father's name, or the occupation.)

25

evening the breath of a slave fanned the flames with the urgent whisper, "Sire, remember the Athenians."

THE IONIAN GREEKS

The Ionians, who lived on the coast of Asia Minor and the adjoining islands, had produced some of the leading poets and thinkers of the Greek world. Thales of Miletus (640–546 B.C.) predicted an eclipse of the sun and introduced geometry to the Greeks. Pythagoras of Samos (c. 500) won fame as a philosopher and mathematician, although it is not now thought that he discovered the geometrical truth which bears his name (i.e. that the square on the hypotenuse of a right-angled triangle is equal to the sum of the squares on the other two sides).

Thales was interested in politics as well as mathematics and tried to unite the cities of Ionia into a federation. Each city-state would have remained independent but would have sent representatives to a council to discuss affairs of common interest. This scheme did not succeed. The Ionian cities of the mainland (except for the largest, Miletus) became subject to Lydia, and later, when Cyrus conquered Croesus (p. 21), they all became subject to Persia. Even some of the islands succumbed. Polycrates, the fabulously wealthy tyrant of Samos, whose position was such that he could enter into a treaty with the king of Egypt, was enticed by the Persians onto the mainland and killed (522).

In the year 522 a pretender had seized the throne of Persia and some nobles, of whom Darius was one, joined in assassinating him. They then decided that they would ride out early in the morning and

The Persian Wars

that the one whose horse neighed first after the sun rose should be King. Darius's groom saw to it that his master's horse neighed first and Darius became King of Persia. Neither fate nor the other nobles punished him for cheating in this way. He ruled Persia until 485, by no means incompetently. He divided his empire into twenty *satrapies*, each governed by an official called a *satrap*. An efficient postal service made it possible for him to keep in close touch. (It was three months' march from Sardis to Susa, Darius's capital, but relays of messengers could do the journey in a week.)

The Ionian Greeks, however, saw things differently. They were governed by tyrants approved by the satrap and had to pay tribute. Finally they organized a revolt and sought help from the cities of mainland Greece. This was how it came about that an Athenian contingent helped to burn Sardis and thus attracted the notice of Darius. When therefore (494) the Ionian revolt was finally put down and the great city of Miletus had been destroyed, Darius "remembered the Athenians". His first expedition against them (492) had to turn back because of the damage done to the fleet in a storm, but in 490 two of his commanders succeeded in crossing the Aegean and landing an army on the plain of Marathon, about twenty-six miles from Athens. With them was the former tyrant Hippias.

MARATHON

Both Sparta and Athens were determined to fight,—so determined that they had behaved outrageously towards Persian ambassadors who had visited them to demand submission. The traditional way of doing this was to ask for "earth and water", but when the ambassadors made this demand in Athens they were thrown into the pit where criminals were put. "Get earth from there", yelled the citizens. At Sparta the ambassadors were plunged into a well. "Get water from there", they were told. Throughout history the person of an ambassador has been held sacred and if the Persians had won at Marathon the Greeks would no doubt have been quick to attribute defeat to the anger of the gods, aroused by Spartan and Athenian insolence.

However, when news of the Persian landing reached Athens, nobody was worrying about how the Persian ambassadors had been treated. There were two vitally important things to be done. An army had to be put into the field and the Spartans had to be summoned.

The story of the summoning of the Spartans is famous but strange. It says that a runner called Pheidippides made the journey (140 miles) on foot in two days. Seventy miles a day. We would consider that quite good going on a bicycle. Perhaps he was given a lift for part of the way. Why not have sent a horseman? The fact that a runner was preferred is a reminder of the hilliness of Greece and of the independence of the city-states. Nobody was interested in building a good road and making the journey from Athens to Sparta as easy as the journey from Susa to Sardis. On the contrary, it was in the interest of both Athenians and Spartans to keep the route rough.

The hardships of his hurried journey were a load which Pheidippides could bear. But the news he had to carry back was heart-breaking. The Spartans were

A hoplite. He wears a metal cuirass over his chest and greaves to protect his lower legs. His spear, used for thrusting, not throwing, was about 9 ft. long. A hoplite had to pay for his armour and a servant carried it to the battlefield for him. He fought in a long line, eight deep, with overlapping shields, called a 'phalanx'.

observing a religious festival and could not march until the moon was full—several days later. So except for the help of a small force from their neighbours, the Plataeans, the Athenians had to face the Persians alone.

The bulk of the Greek force consisted of *hoplites*. Facing them, on lower ground near the sea, were a far greater number of Persian light troops, armed with slings or javelins, and archers. The Athenian general, Miltiades, put more men on the wings than in the centre. As the long line plunged down hill and crashed against the Persians, its weak centre was held; but the wings pressed on—

wards and inwards, until a large part of the Persian force was surrounded. Overpowered, they retreated towards the shore. The Greeks followed and cut down many of them as they clambered on board their ships.

The arrival of news of a great victory is more exciting than the victory itself. Soldiers and sailors do not know the exact moment at which a battle is won, but for those who are waiting at home the messenger from the field has a short and exciting message. It is either "we have won" or "we have lost". No one at the time seems to have described how the news of victory at Marathon reached Athens, but hundreds of years later someone had the idea of saying that Pheidippides had brought it. This story became more popular than the story of Pheidippides's run to Sparta. It ended with Pheidippides reaching Athens exhausted and falling down dead with the words "Rejoice! We win!" and it was made into a poem by Robert Browning.

So when, in A.D. 1896, the first modern Olympic games were held at Athens, a 26 mile race was included and called the "Marathon". The first "Marathon" was run from Marathon to Athens and the winner was not a famous athlete but a Greek shepherd. After that the word gradually passed into the English language so that any long-lasting test of endurance has come to be referred to as a "Marathon".

The arrival of the news is therefore more effectively commemorated today than the victory itself. Forget the cheering crowds in Athens for a moment and look at the battlefield. It is early afternoon and the Persians have fled to their ships. The victorious Athenians are resting (though not for long, as we shall see) among the dead of both sides—192 of their countrymen and 6,400 Persians. How did they manage to win this spectacular victory?

The answer must be that their morale was better. They were fighting near their homes and for their homes. They were also fighting for their new form of government, the beginnings of democracy, which Cleisthenes had given them in place of the ruthless rule of Hippias. And there was a feeling of David and Goliath about the whole affair. The Persian Giant had been thought invincible until now; the Athenians were on their mettle. Perhaps they fought all the better because the Spartans had not come.

The danger of the return of Hippias was great. In spite of their losses the Persians still had a considerable force on board their ships and Hippias was with them. It is said that he was waiting for a signal and that suddenly he saw it. High in the hills above the battlefield a shield caught the fierce flash of the Mediterranean sun. The man who held it was in the pay of Hippias and his party. His message was: "Sail to Athens now".

The Persians sailed, but the Athenians were ready for them. Instead of a defenceless city full of old men, women and children the Persians found that the army had already returned from Marathon and stood ready to meet them once again. (It is this great march immediately after the battle rather than the legendary haste of Pheidippides that is worth commemorating.) The Persians did not want another battle, so they turned back, carrying old Hippias and his hopes away from Athens for the last time.

After a battle there is a great deal of clearing up to be done. A small part of the Athenian force had been left behind to do this. The general in command was Aristides, "the Just". There was no fear of his taking any of the rich Persian spoil for himself. He had gained a reputation for scrupulous honesty, for putting country before self and for modest behaviour. These qualities were rare. Perhaps as he returned to Athens after completing his task at Marathon, he felt that he had a good chance of occupying a powerful position such as had been held by Cleisthenes, whom he had known and admired.

Far from it. A few years later Aristides was ostracised. On the day when the votes were cast it is said that an illiterate citizen, who did not even know Aristides by sight, came up to him and asked for help in marking the piece of broken pottery which served as a voting paper. The citizen wanted "Aristides" written on his. The owner of the name was a little surprised and asked the citizen whether Aristides had injured him in any way. "Oh no," was the answer. "I haven't even met him. But I'm tired of hearing him called 'The Just'." Aristides did not argue but wrote his name on the piece of pottery. If he had had less high principles and more sense of humour he would have written the name of his rival—Themistocles.

Themistocles was pushing and boastful. In the company of artistic people he said, with slimy mock-modesty: "I'm sorry I can't play any musical instrument. All I can do is to make a small city into a great one." When a visitor from one of the Aegean islands belittled the fame Themistocles had won and said it belonged not to him but to Athens, Themistocles quickly retorted: "True, I would not have been famous had I lived on your island, but neither would you have been, if you had lived in Athens." He had a spoilt young son, whom he used to call the most powerful person in Greece, explaining: "The Athenians command the rest of Greece, I command the Athenians, your Mother commands me and you command your mother." Yet he was popular. He knew how to flatter his audience, whereas Aristides probably did not bother. He was also extremely far-sighted. In the year when his rival was ostracised there was a surplus from the state-owned silver mines at Laurium (see map p. 16), which would normally have been distributed among the citizens. But Themistocles persuaded them to use it instead to build two hundred triremes (opposite). These warships saved Greece from Persia's second attack and laid the foundations of a naval supremacy which was to make Athens rich and famous.

THE SECOND PERSIAN INVASION

Darius I died in 486. In the last years of his life he had no need of the slave who had whispered, "Sire, remember the Athenians." He remembered Marathon all too well and was making preparations for another attack on Greece. These preparations were continued after Darius's death by his son Xerxes. By the year 480 an enormous force had assembled at Sardis and a fleet was ready to sail in support.

This "Persian" army and fleet was in fact made up of contingents drawn from all over the vast Persian Empire, including

Trireme—a Greek warship, 150 ft. long, 16 ft. broad. The name means that she carried three banks of oars, but it is not known how the 170 rowers were arranged. They were poorer citizens, not slaves, and therefore received pay. A flute-player kept them in time. Steering was done by two oars in the stern. A mainsail was carried for running before the wind. A speed of 7 knots could be kept up for some time and journeys of 50 miles a day were not unusual. The commander, a 'trierarch', had to be rich, since he paid for the maintenance and repair of the ship.

Ionian Greeks. The march out of Sardis was a gorgeous and gigantic pageant. Dark Ethiopians had come in leopard skins from their mysterious country in the far south. Indians in a light cotton uniform represented the easternmost territories of the Empire. From the north came Scythian bowmen in long trousers and pointed caps. Xerxes himself rode in a chariot with picked Persian cavalry and spearmen marching in front and behind.

Xerxes might well feel confident. The expedition had been carefully planned. Food and supplies had been collected along the route, and a canal had been cut through the promontory of Mount Athos, so that the fleet might avoid the stormy passage round the end of it. Even the problem of crossing the Hellespont had been solved, though not without some unpleasantness. Two bridges consisting of hundreds of ships placed side by side had been built across the mile-wide strait, but they were soon destroyed by a storm. This infuriated Xerxes, who decided that the Hellespont should be brutally punished. Its waters were to receive three hundred lashes, to be branded, loaded with chains and ceremonially cursed. The penalty imposed on the builders of the bridges was less complicated. They simply had their heads cut off. Their successors were either more competent or luckier with the weather. The bridges they built held firm.

Under the shadow of this undignified outburst the mighty army moved northwards to make the crossing. On the way they passed between two halves of a man, impaled on either side of the road. This man had done nothing wrong, but his father had been indiscreet. Finding that he had won the King's favour by his lavish entertainment of the army, the father had been bold enough to ask what he thought was a small favour. "I have five sons," he said. "They have all been ordered to take part in this expedition against Greece. Might not the eldest stay behind to help me?" The whole army knew the answer Xerxes had given, as they marched between the halves of the eldest son's corpse.

Xerxes was not a leader who inspired devotion; but if numbers alone could win, his success seemed assured. The army was gigantic. Seven days and seven nights were needed for its various contingents to ride or march or be lashed across the boat-bridges into Europe.

The threat was so serious that the Greek city-states for once succeeded in putting a united force into the field. They even hoped for help from their fellow-countrymen in Sicily, but Gelo, the tyrant of Syracuse, insisted that he must be supreme commander if he came. Neither the Spartans nor the Athenians were willing to have his help on those terms. He could probably not have come anyway, since his own state was threatened by the Phoenicians of Carthage. (The Phoenicians of the eastern Mediterranean were subjects of Xerxes and he had thus been able to influence their Carthaginian kinsmen.)

No help therefore came from Sicily, nor were the Greeks of Ionia and the islands able to help their mother-country. On the contrary, they supplied part of the Persian fleet.

One of the reasons why the Greeks lived in city-states, independent of one another, was the mountainous nature of their country (refer to maps on pages 2 and 16). These mountains, however, now helped their defence. So did their jagged, islanded coastline. An invader of Greece whether on land or sea had to go through narrow places where great numbers did not necessarily give a great advantage. Narrow places proved fatal to Xerxes.

THERMOPYLAE

The first narrow place where the Persians might have been held was the pass of Tempe in the north of Thessaly. A force was sent there but withdrew when news came that the Persians might take another route and outflank them. Thessaly was thus abandoned to the Persians; but they were not to be allowed farther south without a fight. The only route lay through the pass of Thermopylae. Here Leonidas the Spartan, who was Commander in Chief of the Greek forces, decided to make a stand, while the combined Greek fleet kept watch near Artemisium on the Persian ships, which were sailing along the coast in support of their army.

Thermopylae is still a position vital to the defence of Greece, but it is no longer a narrow pass. The sea has retreated. When Leonidas and his men took up their position it came close to the foot of the mountains, leaving only a narrow passage between.

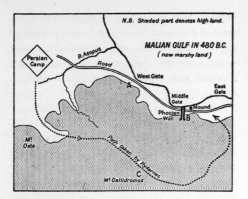

*Thermopylae: Greeks' first stand (A);
last stand (B); Phocians (C)*

Xerxes was surprised when he was told that the pass was held. He was inclined to be contemptuous when a spy reported that the enemy troops were engaged in gymnastics and were combing their hair. In fact the spy had been looking at the cream of the Greek force—three hundred Spartans. It was the Spartan custom to wear long hair and to prepare for battle in this apparently lackadaisical fashion. These same men had been warned that the arrows of the Persians would be so numerous as to darken the sun, to which one of them had replied: "Excellent. We shall have our fight in the shade then."

Xerxes did not attack for four days, since he still expected the Greeks to retreat without fighting. On the fifth day however he sent a force with orders to capture the Greeks and bring them back alive. This force failed. They brought no Greeks back alive. They would have been glad to bring back their own dead, but there were too many of them. On the sixth day, therefore, the bravest of the Persian troops, who were called the Immortals, hurled themselves against the Greeks; but even they could not break through.

It was then that a Greek traitor came to Xerxes offering to show the path over the mountains which would make it possible—he hoped—to take the Greeks in the rear. The offer was eagerly accepted and a Persian force set out.

Leonidas had not forgotten this path. On the contrary, it was guarded by a thousand Phocians who lived in that part of the country and who had volunteered for this particular duty. A commander could hardly have done more to secure his position—a thousand Phocian men guarding a narrow path and knowing that if they failed in their duty their homes would be the first to suffer. Yet it was these men who fled at the first sight of the Persians and let them through.

When Leonidas heard what had happened, he realised that his position was hopeless and sent away most of his force. Then, with his three hundred Spartans and some others, he fought once more in the pass and died there.

Thermopylae was a Persian victory but the Persians paid so dearly for it that succeeding generations regarded Leonidas as one of the saviours of Greece. The nobility of his men has made posterity forget the ignoble Spartan system which produced them. And why not? For this brief moment of Greek history Sparta is the hero.

But the three hundred did not think of themselves as fighting for an ideal. They were simply doing their duty. So, when Simonides of Ceos (556–467) composed their epitaph, it was not of a fight for freedom, but of obedience which he wrote:

Make known among the Spartans, passer-by,
That here, obedient to their laws, we lie.

"WOODEN WALLS" AND SALAMIS

After Thermopylae the Spartans were only interested in defending the Peloponnese. Their next line of defence was across the Isthmus of Corinth. The atmosphere on the two sides of that line was now very different. Much of the Peloponnese was still far from the war. At Olympia the four-yearly games were taking place as usual. (Who on earth was free to attend them? one wonders.) North of the Corinthian gulf, however, townsmen and countrymen alike knew that the Persian army would be on top of them any day now. Knowing this, what did they do?

The men of Delphi routed the Persian force which hoped to plunder the treasures of their sanctuary. They were helped by a storm and probably by some hocus-pocus arranged by the resourceful priests of Apollo. The men of Bœotia, with its capital, Thebes, put up no opposition and submitted to Persian occupation. The Athenians evacuated Attica, moved their families over to Salamis, Aegina or the Peloponnese and waited to see what Themistocles and his ships would do.

Themistocles had been with the Greek fleet at Artemisium, opposing the Persians at sea, while Leonidas fought them on land. He then moved south, inscribing propaganda slogans on the rocks, where he hoped the Ionians in the Persian fleet would read them and be moved to desert. But when the Persian fleet later passed that way (there had been a period of shore leave for the sailors to inspect and exult over the Spartan dead) no Ionian showed any sign of wanting to change sides.

The Persian army advanced through Attica and entered Athens. The Delphic oracle had said that Athens would be kept safe by her "wooden walls" and a few diehards, refusing to take part in the evacuation, remained behind a wooden barricade on the Acropolis. They learned too late that they had misinterpreted the oracle. Their resistance was overcome and Xerxes burned Athens. Themistocles and his sailors could now be sure that their ships were the only "wooden walls" which stood between the Athenians and annihilation.

Unfortunately, although Athens had supplied by far the largest number of ships (180) to the Greek fleet, the admiral-in-chief was a Spartan. Athens had not yet the prestige to persuade other states to serve under her. At sea, as on land, a Spartan had to be in charge.

Spartans or Corinthians could view the Athenian refugees and the smoking ruins of their homes with equanimity. In their hearts they were probably rather relieved. What mattered to them was the defence of the Isthmus. As far as they were concerned, the sooner the fleet left the better. Themistocles, however, was sure that the narrows between Salamis and the mainland were the best place in which to fight the more cumbersome and more numerous Persian ships. Having failed to persuade his allies, he finally got his way by sending to Xerxes a trusted slave, who gave warning that the Greek fleet intended

Persian soldier

the Greeks won. This was in September of the year 480.

The victory at Salamis was splendid and noble men were there. Aristides, his exile shortened because of the emergency, plunged ashore at the head of the first landing party. Aeschylus, the poet, a veteran of Marathon, was probably with him. He put it all into a play, a tragedy called the *Persians*, in which Themistocles is not mentioned. It is Zeus whom Aeschylus thanks for the glorious victory.

Xerxes had watched the battle from a throne, which had been placed for him on a hill above the narrows. When it was over he decided to leave Greece. The remains of the fleet and part of the army moved back towards the Hellespont, where the bridges of boats were still intact. The rest of the Persian army attacked again in the following year (479) but was defeated at Plataea. Then they too retreated.

The Persians never returned to Greece, but some years later they welcomed a distinguished Greek visitor and made him extremely comfortable. He was Themistocles. Like Hippias the ex-tyrant, he had made his homeland too hot for him and wanted breathing space to plan a comeback. In time he lost heart and took poison —an undignified death for the victor of Salamis. So Athens was set on the way to power by a talented traitor.

to slip away. On hearing this the Persians sent an Egyptian squadron to close the channel of escape between Salamis and the mainland. Then the Persian fleet sailed in, thinking the Greeks were trapped.

But it was the Persians who were trapped. Their numbers were no advantage in the confined space and the Greek ships, which were lighter and more skilfully manœuvred, soon began to get the upper hand. It was not an easy victory. Fighting went on all day. But in the end

AESCHYLUS

Play-acting had been developing at Athens since Peisistratus had introduced the Dionysia and the Panathenaea festivals; but to call it play-acting in the early stages gives a false impression. It was more like open air opera and ballet with

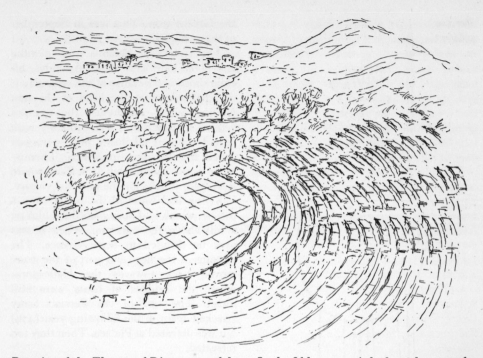

Remains of the Theatre of Dionysus at Athens. In the fifth century it had wooden seats for perhaps 17,000 people and those in the highest rows had a splendid view seawards. During the performance of the "Persians" (p. 37) they could actually see the stretch of water on which the battle of Salamis had been fought. In the foreground were the chorus and behind a low stage for the principal actors. There was a small wooden building at the back of the stage, but very little scenery and no curtain. Entry cost only a few obols. Women were admitted.

a strong religious flavour. Originally there was a "chorus" of fifty men who chanted and danced in a dignified way. In the intervals an actor recited. Aeschylus added a second actor and the two actors, as well as conversing with each other, conversed with the chorus or its leader. All wore masks and impressive robes.

Several plays were performed one after the other and the performance lasted all day. Later there were three actors, each of whom could play more than one part, and a chorus of only fifteen. There were plenty of female parts, but they were always played by men.

The little we know of the music makes it certain that we would have found it monotonous. It was usually provided by a man playing a kind of flute.

Aeschylus grew up to the sound of poetry, but none of it was Athenian. Homer was Ionian; Hesiod was a Boeotian (see p. 9); so was Pindar (c. 522–442), who wrote odes in honour of victors in the Olympic games. Sappho, the woman lyric poet (c. 600 B.C.), was a native of Lesbos. Simonides, as we have seen (p. 33) was from Ceos. There were many others, from the islands, from the mainland and even from Sparta. Aeschylus, however, is the first great Athenian poet of whom we know.

The *Persians* was exceptional among tragedies in dealing with recent history. The characters in most tragedies were drawn from legend or the distant past. But Aeschylus was interested in the sin of getting above oneself, of getting too big for one's boots, and the conduct of Xerxes was an excellent example of this.

Unfortunately neither Aeschylus nor Athens took the lesson to heart. At the Great Dionysia in 468, Sophocles, who had been only fifteen at the time of Salamis, won first prize in the drama contest; whereupon Aeschylus left Athens in disgust and lived in Sicily for some years, though he later wrote finer plays than ever (e.g. *Agamemnon*, 458).

THESEUS COMES HOME

The annual festival of the Great Dionysia, in March of the year 468, was not only remarkable for the victory of twenty-seven year old Sophocles over the honoured and battle-scarred Aeschylus, who was now approaching sixty. There was something else.

Owing to the excitement which the competition between youth and age had aroused, the official whose duty it was to appoint the judges had not yet dared to do so. He was about to solve the problem in the way that Athens solved many prob-lems—by drawing lots—when Cimon, an aristocrat, politician and admiral, entered the great open-air theatre with nine of his senior officers. They had just returned from a naval expedition, during which they had subdued the island of Scyros, the supposed burial place of Theseus. An oracle had said that the body of Theseus should be brought back to Athens and Cimon had brought it (or someone else's; there were no archaeologists to put awkward questions). Cimon was therefore the hero of the hour.

The official in charge stood by the altar. (These drama festivals, you will remember, were religious ceremonies, the god on this occasion being Dionysus.) With relief the official saw Cimon and his officers come in. Certain that his choice would be popular he led them to the altar and administered the judges' oath. It was their decision which sent Aeschylus off to Sicily in a rage.

For our present purpose the point of interest in this story is the huge coffin, alleged to contain the body of the mighty Theseus, which the Athenians had greeted with such rejoicing. That sort of demonstration over a legendary hero takes place either when a people is in great danger, or when they become ambitious. Now although Athens was still at war with Persia, the Persians had left Greece. The Athenians were no longer in great danger. Were they becoming ambitious?

THE CONFEDERACY OF DELOS

About the same time as the land victory at Plataea (479) the Greek fleet had beaten the Persians at Mycale on the coast of Asia Minor (478) and now that they were absolutely sure which was the winning side the Ionian Greeks of the coast and the islands gradually decided to change sides again. But they needed help. Persian garrisons had to be driven out.

The Spartans might have undertaken this. They had been the acknowledged leaders of Greece on land and during the campaign against Xerxes. But the Spartans were not enterprising enough and they were always afraid that the downtrodden Helots might revolt, while their masters were campaigning outside the Peloponnese. So it was Athens which seized the opportunity and formed a confederacy of Aegean towns and islands for defence against Persia. Some larger islands such as Chios, Lesbos and Samos provided ships, but most members of the league contributed money.

Aristides, old now but still renowned for honesty, decided how much each of the confederates should pay and the money was kept in earthenware jars at Apollo's shrine on the island of Delos. From the first Athens was very much the leading partner and imposed strict discipline. When in 467, the year after the triumphant return of Theseus in his coffin, the island of Naxos tried to leave the Confederacy, it was forced to continue

These sculptured lions, which can still be seen on the island of Delos, were already old when the tribute of Athens's allies was stored there

as a contributor. Athens insisted that since no Aegean city-state could help benefiting from the league's activities, no state should be allowed to stay out of it. This is a reasonable enough argument, but one might have expected it to be used by the Ionians against Athens, rather than the other way round. The Ionians, after all, were nearest to the Persian danger. But it was Athens which took the lead.

Athens was becoming ambitious. Urged by Themistocles, she had quickly rebuilt her fortifications and had fortified her new harbour, the Peiraeus, after Plataea. Now (about 457), long walls were built between the city and the coast, so that the city could not be surrounded and cut off from her ships by an enemy on land. These developments did not pass unnoticed at Sparta.

THE ATHENIAN EMPIRE

Cimon was rich and pro-Spartan, but generous. He kept open house and invited the public to make use of his garden and grounds. It was said that he got riches that he might use them, and used them that he might get honour by them. This was in fact the course which Athens herself now began to adopt; but Cimon was not destined to steer her along it.

He had a rival, Pericles. In 461 the queer process of ostracism was once again brought into operation. (For the events leading up to this see p. 44.) Every citizen scratched a name on a piece of broken pottery. When the count was made it became clear that fear of Sparta meant more to the Athenians than the use of Cimon's garden. Cimon had to go. For the next thirty years Athens was guided by Pericles.

In 454 things went badly for Athens.

Pericles. He wears the 'Corinthian' type of helmet, which could be pulled down to cover the whole face for fighting.

She lost 200 ships which had been sent on an expedition as far afield as Egypt. What if the Phoenician vassals of Persia should choose this moment to raid Delos and rob the treasury of the League? They must not be given the chance. Once again, just as at the time when she had prevented the secession of Naxos, the action taken by Athens was very reasonable and at the same time very advantageous to herself. She removed the League's accumulated wealth from Delos to Athens. Finally, in 451, rights of citizenship were restricted to men whose father and mother were Athenian born. This limited the number of those who were entitled to share in the spoils of what could now be called, not a confederacy, but an empire.

While Athens thus became more autocratic towards her former allies, her own system of government, as far as full citizens were concerned, became more democratic. Pericles went farther than Solon or Cleisthenes. The Assembly was now made the ruling body, assisted by the Council of five hundred, which carried on business between the Assembly's meetings. The old aristocratic council of the Areopagus lost almost all its powers. The archonship was thrown open to citizens even of the lowest class, and archons, councillors and jurors henceforth received pay, so that no one should be excluded from serving owing to poverty. These were some of the 'perks' of empire which made Athenians anxious to restrict full citizenship. Another was the chance of inclusion in a *cleruchy*, a colony sent out to settle at some point which was strategically important to Athens, e.g., on the trade route along which corn supplies reached Athens from the Black Sea.

The ten generals, elected annually by the Assembly, continued to exercise more influence than the archon, who was chosen by lot. It was on his election as president of the ten generals that Pericles depended for his power, year after year. This power, although arrived at democratically, became so great as to give rise to the remark that Athens was "in theory a democracy but in fact under the rule of her first citizen".

In 447 peace (The "Peace of Callias") was finally made with Persia. That was the time to argue, as a few Athenians and many League members did, that the Confederacy had now served its purpose. It had been founded to complete the liberation of Greeks from Persians, which Salamis had begun. The islands and the cities of Ionia were now free. Why not dissolve the League?

The official answer was still the same. Peace or no peace, the Persian danger was still there and the Athenian navy was the best guarantee against its flaring up again. The navy protected the whole Aegean; so the whole Aegean should contribute towards it; and as to expenditure of any surplus, after the navy had been supplied, would not all members of the League benefit if their capital city was beautified?

But the real reason why Athens did not dissolve the Confederacy was simple. Athenians liked getting the tribute. Workmen were now engaged on the early stages of the Parthenon, the new temple of Athena which was to overlook the city. Who would pay them if the tribute stopped?

THE FATHER OF HISTORY

Two years later (445), if tradition can be trusted, the Athenians must have felt more self-confident than ever; for it was then that Herodotus came to Athens, read aloud his history of the Persian wars, and was given a reward. That the Athenians should have listened with interest as well as gratification is not surprising. The historian had done full justice to their distinguished part in the Persian Wars and in addition his work (9 books in all) contained all sorts of interesting details about countries like Egypt and Scythia (south Russia) which were only remotely connected with the war. Herodotus had travelled widely and produced a combined guide book and history covering most of the known world. No one had ever done anything of this sort before.

"My duty is to report all that is said", wrote Herodotus, "but I am not obliged to believe it all alike." There is no doubt that people told him some odd stories. But the bulk of Herodotus is reliable. His

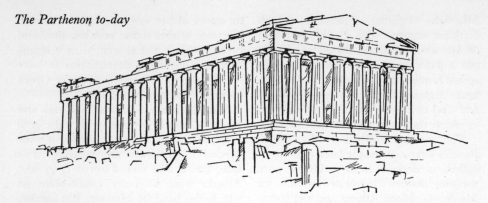

History ends in the year 478. We have no detailed continuous account of the period 478–432.

In 443 the Athenians founded a colony at Thurii in southern Italy, and there Herodotus ended his days. Just when he went there is uncertain. We do not know whether he was still at Athens in 441 when a new dramatist, Euripides, won his first success, or in 440 when his friend Sophocles won a prize for his play *Antigone* (the name of the heroine).

The *Antigone* is a tender play, which sets the audience worrying about how difficult it is to do one's duty—loyalty to a friend may mean disloyalty to one's country. This is a very real problem, though one best not pondered by soldiers. Their first duty must be unquestioning obedience to orders. Yet on the strength of this play the Athenians made Sophocles a general, and off he went, serving under Pericles, to help to bring the recalcitrant island of Samos to heel (439).

All this would not have surprised Herodotus as it surprises us. Still, it would be interesting to have his account of Athens at this time, when she had reached the height of her power and glory.

THE PARTHENON

In the year 437 the Parthenon, which had been begun ten years before, was far enough advanced to contain a gigantic statue of Athena by the sculptor Pheidias. Enough of the Parthenon still survives to give an idea of how it must have looked when it was new, and a visit to the British Museum will fill in the details. Here some of the sculptured figures which adorned the temple may be seen. They are known as the 'Elgin Marbles' because Lord Elgin brought them back from Greece in 1802–4 to save them from the Turks, who then ruled the Greeks (p. 67). Now that that danger is past, the Greeks would like them back. But Pheidias, who supervised their construction, would not necessarily have regretted that Athens had lost them. The Athenians treated him very badly. After his work was finished he constructed the statue of Zeus at Olympia (one of the 'seven wonders of the world') and thereafter returned to Athens. Enemies of Pericles, whose friend Pheidias was, then tried to attack Pericles through him. He was accused of impiety. It was alleged that he had introduced his own likeness and that of Pericles into the scene of

Athenians fighting Amazons (tough mythical women) with which the shield of Athena's statue was decorated. It was not a flattering portrait. He had represented himself as a bald old man about to heave a stone. But he was put in prison and died of disease there in 432, the year in which the Parthenon was finished.

The name 'Parthenon', by which Pericles's famous temple later came to be called, is derived from a Greek word meaning 'maiden'. It was dedicated to the Maiden Goddess, Athena and the gigan-

There were three positions for sculpture on the Parthenon—the frieze, of which the picture on page 51 shows a small part, the metopes and the pediments. Some sculpture is still in position, some is in the British and other museums, Originally it was coloured.

tic statue of her was its greatest treasure. No trace of this statue now remains, and perhaps this is just as well, since it seems from the surviving descriptions to have been not at all in keeping with the Greek ideal of "nothing in excess".

The statue was about 40 feet high and made of wood covered with thin gold plate, which could be removed if it were needed to replenish the treasury. The face, hands and feet were of ivory and Athena wore an ivory breast-plate on which the head of Medusa, the gorgon, was carved. Her shield bore the unfortunate scene of the Athenians fighting the Amazons which had brought Pheidias into trouble. In her right hand she held a statue of Victory, itself some 6 ft. high. Even her sandals told a story. On them were wrought pictures of the mythical battle between the Centaurs (half man, half horse) and the Lapiths. Perhaps the effect was splendid. One must not forget that this statue was the work of Pheidias. But it certainly sounds rather vulgar.

The year 432, when the Parthenon was finally completed and Pheidias died, was the year in which events occurred which led to the outbreak of the disastrous Peloponnesian War.

THUCYDIDES

When Herodotus read his history in public (p. 40), it is said that a youth called Thucydides was so moved that he burst into tears. Herodotus congratulated the young man's father upon having so appreciative a son.

Thucydides grew to be a rich man. He owned gold mines in Thrace. During the Peloponnesian War he commanded a squadron of Athenian ships but, having

The statue of Athena in the Parthenon may have looked like this. None of it survives.

author's aim was different. He was determined to write what we would now call scientific history. He took care about dates, grouping each year's events together. He checked facts and weighed up one account of an event against another. He travelled in order to collect information and during his exile had access to both sides in the struggle.

On the other hand, when he came to the reporting of speeches, Thuycides made a point of not being scientific. The speeches he put into the mouths of many of his characters were far more than a digest of what had been said. They contained the historian's own views on why men had acted as they did and what were the rights and wrongs of the question. These views were often wise.

Thus, though the Peloponnesian War was small in comparison with many of the wars of ancient history, we know a great deal about it. Further, because of the quality of Thucydides's writing, we can *feel* a great deal about it. Though he was not himself a tragic poet, Thucydides well understood the tragedian's business. His readers look on appalled as Athens sails towards her doom.

WHY DID ATHENS FIGHT SPARTA?

failed to accomplish the mission assigned to him, he went into exile (424). He used his enforced leisure to work on a history of the war which he had planned. He only reached 411 (the War went on till 404), but he produced a remarkable work. It is less chatty than that of Herodotus because the

In spite of the fact that they had fought as allies against Persia, Sparta and Athens did not like each other any better when the war was over. In 478, when the Athenians started to rebuild their fortifications, Sparta objected and Themistocles had to arrange for negotiations to drag on until the walls were finished. There followed the Spartan failure to lead the Ionians against Persia, while Athens founded the Delian League.

Athenian Alliance

Spartan Alliance

M.t Pangaeus
Amphipolis
Eion
THASOS

Olynthus
Potidaea
Mende

CORCYRA
Sybota

THESSALY

AMBRACIA
Anactorium Olpae
LEUCAS
Stratus Heraclea N.LOCRIS
ACARNANIA
AETOLIA
Oeniadae Naupactus S.LOCRIS
CEPHALLENIA
PHOCIS
BOEOTIA Delium
Chaeronea
Siphae Thebes
ACHAEA Plataea Decelea
Phyle
Elis Megara Athens
Corinth ATTICA
ZACYNTHUS
ARGOLID Aegina
Argos Methana Sunium
Mantinea
ARCADIA
Tegea
MESSENIA
Sparta
Pylos
Methone LACONIA
MELOS
EUBOEA

50 Miles

CYTHERA

In 464 the long dreaded revolt of the Helots began, following an earthquake which had laid the town of Sparta in ruins. After some savage fighting the Helots were forced to take refuge on the hill of Ithome, where they managed to hold out for the next ten years. The Helot revolt provided a chance for Athens either to win Spartan gratitude by helping to capture Ithome, or to take advantage of her old enemy's embarrassing situation. She tried both.

Since Cimon (p. 39), was pro-Spartan and an aristocrat, it was natural for him to support an upper against a lower class. He persuaded the Athenians to send him with a strong force in response to the Spartan appeal for help (462). But a quarrel arose when the force reached Ithome and the Spartans asked the Athenians to leave again. This insult enraged the Athenians. Cimon was ostracised and Athens formed an alliance with Argos, Sparta's traditional rival in the Peloponnese. When the Helots finally surrendered (454), on terms which allowed them to leave the Peloponnese, Athens settled them at Naupactus, a harbour commanding the passage up the Corinthian gulf.

Sparta was still the most formidable land power in Greece and in 445 a Spartan army reached the walls of Athens, but there was no battle. On this occasion, Pericles and the Spartan King concluded a thirty years peace. Athens recognised the supremacy of Sparta and her allies on land; Sparta accepted Athenian supremacy at sea. This was all very well as long as no further disagreement arose; but as soon as a disagreement or rather two disagreements did arise, the old question had to be faced again. Who was going to give way? Neither Sparta nor Athens was willing.

Thucydides said that the real cause of the war was the growing power of Athens and the resultant alarm at Sparta. He then went on to describe the 'occasions'— the incidents which preceded the outbreak of war. There were two.

THE PELOPONNESIAN WAR BEGINS

In the first place Athens insisted on backing Corcyra in a quarrel with Corinth (435). Corcyra was a Corinthian colony and the mother-city resented interference in the dispute, particularly since it brought Athenian ships round to the western coast of Greece where they could interfere with the trade route to southern Italy.

The second trouble-centre was also a Corinthian colony, though a tribute-paying member of the Athenian Empire —Potidaea in Thrace. Now that Athens saw trouble brewing with Corinth she insisted (432) that Potidaea should get rid of the Corinthian magistrates who came year by year from the mother-city, should give hostages, and knock down the city wall. The Potidaeans then revolted. They received support from Corinth, while the Athenians sent a force to subdue them.

Corinth was a member of the Spartan alliance, so the Peloponnesian War had in fact begun. The only remaining question was whether it could be localized— confined to N.W. and N.E. Greece. The Spartans called together their allies—all the Peloponnesian states (except Argos); Corinth, Megara and Boeotia (except for Plataea)—and decided for general war.

Pericles on his side made no great effort to preserve the peace. On the contrary, he insulted and injured the Peloponnesian alliance by excluding all Megarian produce from the Athenian Empire.

He did not want war in order to obtain personal success as a general. He had had plenty of that when he was younger, and he was now over sixty. But he wanted Athens to remain powerful and he believed that she must therefore not only protect what she already had—her Aegean Empire, but must also reach out westwards towards Italy and Sicily. Rather than abandon his plans he was prepared to go to war. Perhaps too he felt that, if there was going to be a war sooner or later, it ought to be sooner, so that he could run it. He had made his plans.

In May 431 the Spartan army marched into Attica. Pericles intended to avoid a land battle with the Spartans. This plan was not popular, but the Athenians accepted it. They had been accepting plans made by Pericles for some forty years.

Amongst the loudest opponents of the plan, naturally, were young men who hoped to distinguish themselves in battle. Ever since they could remember they had been excited and then bored by stories of how bravely grandfather had fought at Marathon. Now they wanted their chance. They were angry when they heard they were not going to get it.

But those who suffered most were the families who had to abandon their farms. Some went over to Euboea, with their goats and cattle, but many crowded into Athens, where they had to camp out in the open space between the Long Walls. There had not been time for them to harvest their corn, and the Spartans took it. This did not mean that Athens starved, since even in peacetime she depended a great deal on imported corn from cleruchies (see p. 40). But it was a bitter blow to the farmers. Luckily, in this first year, the Spartans only stayed six weeks. Systematic destruction needed longer than that.

Pericles retaliated by sending a hundred ships with hoplites on board to raid the coast of the Peloponnese, but their activities were cold comfort for the men and women who had to return to plundered farms. In the autumn, however, some of them did finally have the satisfaction of seeing an army march out of Athens and return after plundering the territory of Megara.

WHAT DID ATHENIANS FEEL ABOUT DEATH?

When Aeschylus, in his play, the *Persians*, thanked the gods for the victory of Salamis, he was writing for an audience who still had religious faith. But in the years of prosperity which followed, although bigger statues of the gods and more splendid temples went on being put up, piety did not keep pace. On the contrary, the philosophers argued about the gods, Euripides made jokes about them in his plays, and the ordinary man bothered much less about them, now that life had become so much safer and more prosperous. Women, who on the whole had a thinner time, perhaps worshipped more sincerely. There were of course plenty of religious festivals (e.g., the Panathenaea and the Great Dionysia) and plenty of religious customs (e.g., after dinner men would each pour some wine out of their cups in honour of Zeus) and it must also be remembered how difficult it is in any age to find out people's feelings about religion. This much, however, can be said with certainty: the Athenians who embarked upon the Peloponnesian War were not a pious people.

How then did they face death? Not cheerfully. Even the faith of older generations could not help them. The aged Charon, so ran the story, ferried you across the river Styx to Hades, where you lived out a shadowy, unhappy existence till the end of time. Charon was now a joke; but the dreaded, shadowy eternity remained. No one, except perhaps the select few who took part in the secret Eleusinian Mysteries, had any hope to offer. So the Athenians generally burned their dead, put the ashes in an urn made of pottery, buried it and placed some food for the departed spirit on the grave. Later they put up a gravestone. And that was that.

Men who fell in battle were given a state funeral and a speech was made. In the late autumn of 431, when the first casualties of the Peloponnesian War were buried,

Pericles made the speech. Since he could not offer the mourners any consolation in the form of hope for a life after death, he devoted himself to praise of Athens.

He explained how her democratic government favoured the many instead of the few and her laws afforded equal justice to all. Poverty he said, need not be a bar to advancement; on the contrary, every citizen was expected to be a judge of public affairs. Discussion was regarded as an essential preliminary to action (in some countries, he hinted, obviously thinking of Sparta, discussion was frowned upon).

Again tilting at Sparta, where foreigners were not welcome, he said that Athens was open to all—foreigners might go everywhere and see everything, even if they occasionally abused the privilege. Athenian education too was superior to Spartan; the Spartans imposed a rigorous discipline from childhood, while Athenians grew up in freedom but became every bit as brave.

"In short" he went on (and this is perhaps the most famous passage of the speech, as recorded by Thucydides), "I say that as a city we are the school of Hellas; and I doubt if the world can produce a man, who, where he has only himself to depend upon, is equal to so many emergencies and graced by so happy a versatility as the Athenian. . . . I would have you day by day fix your eyes upon the greatness of Athens, until you become her lovers."

Gradually the mourners were brought to realise the many-sided glory of the city for which their loved ones had died. Men who died for such a city would be famous far beyond its borders. Their deeds would be remembered, wherever brave deeds were remembered. "For" said Pericles, "heroes have the whole world for their tomb."

Thucydides is a splendid historian but he does not always tell us all we want to know. How did the mourners react to this speech? Nobody knows. What we do know is that with all his fine phrases Pericles had not yet spoken one word of real comfort. He had two sons of his own; but he did not say: "I know how you feel." He realised, however, that something more intimate was expected of him, so he said that those fathers who were young enough should beget more children in order to help them forget those they had lost and to help the state.

And a word to the women whose husbands had been killed? Just this—"Don't get yourself talked about among men." Then, with an assurance that the children of the fallen would be brought up at the public expense, the speech ended.

Charon's old boat must have creaked that night, so laden with honour were his sad ghostly passengers. But as the winter sun set over Athens and night covered her splendour there were many who went uncomforted to bed.

HIPPOCRATES AND DISEASE

If death was the end, what could be done to stave it off? Deprived of what we would now call the comforts of religion, could the Athenian at least rely on an efficient medical service?

Herodotus describes a doctor called Democedes who (in the 6th cent.) was hired by three states in turn—Aegina, Athens and Samos—each offering a higher salary than the last. So there may have been some sort of state medical service.

A doctor bleeding a patient into a large flat bowl. Another patient with a bandaged arm waits to be treated. Walking sticks are carried and the men wear the 'himation', a long oblong garment which was wound round the body leaving the right arm bare. There were no pockets. Some things could be carried in the folds of the himation. Small change was carried in the mouth. (Working men and youths wore a belted tunic—chiton. Women wore a larger version of this.)

Army doctors appear as early as the Trojan War, and a wounded Athenian in the Peloponnesian War would be efficiently bandaged. Ointments would be applied, broken limbs set, herbal remedies administered. That was something. But medicine cannot progress without dissection. Unlike the Egyptians, the Greeks did not dissect bodies and find out how they worked.

Hippocrates of Cos was alive at the time of the Peloponnesian War. His careful study of the symptoms of patients suffering from certain diseases (e.g. epilepsy and tape-worm) was an advance

at a time when many people still thought that cures could best be effected by sacrificing to the god Asklepios or lying in his shrine. (See Calder, *The Story of Nursing*.) And Hippocrates may have had a good influence on the behaviour of doctors, e.g., in preventing them revealing private matters which they had learned in the houses of patients. Doctors in Britain still swear what is called the Hippocratic oath, and some of the provisions of this oath may have originated with Hippocrates himself. But we do not hear of his practising dissection. In short, although Greek doctors were famous in the ancient

48

world and made a valuable contribution to medical history, the available medical treatment was crude and surgery hardly existed until Alexandrine times (p. 65).

When, therefore, the Spartans invaded again in the spring of 430 and the country people again overcrowded the city and plague broke out, nobody had any idea what to do about it.

Most people who caught the plague died within a week. Thucydides was one of those who recovered. The symptoms were horrible—headache, inflamed eyes, bad breath, sickness and a raging unquenchable thirst. Ulcers broke out all over the body and sufferers could not bear the touch of clothes. They were unable to sleep. It was as if a slow merciless fire was burning inside them and the body was fighting a long battle against it. The battle was one which many—such was their torment—were not sorry to lose.

The war went on and the plague went on with it. As in the previous year, Pericles sent a force to raid the Peloponnese but many of the soldiers and sailors died of the plague. Plague also attacked the army which was still besieging Potidaea.

DEATH OF PERICLES

In Athens morale was low. For the second year in succession the Spartans had been allowed to lay waste the countryside. This alone would have embittered public opinion. But now, in addition, there was the plague. People began to talk about suing for peace. Criticism of Pericles, already sharp enough in the previous year, now reached a point where it had to be answered.

Pericles tried to appeal to the patriotism of the Assembly and then to their common sense. He said: "Let us be frank. What we have established is a kind of dictatorship. Perhaps we were wrong to do so, but we cannot risk turning back now." He pointed out that his policy of avoiding a great land battle and trusting the navy had worked. The only factor he had not foreseen was the plague. How could he have foreseen it?

The fickle Athenians fined Pericles and then, not long afterwards, re-elected him as their general. But he never led them into battle again. In the summer of 429 the Spartans did not invade Attica. They besieged Plataea instead (Athens was bound by treaty to help Plataea, but did not do so. Two years later the town capitulated). In the autumn the Athenian admiral Phormio won a series of victories in the Corinthian Gulf, but by that time Pericles was very ill with a lingering form of the plague. It would soon be his turn for the funeral speech and procession. Soon his bier would be born through the streets preceded by hired mourners and flute players on its way to the pyre and he would lie on it with a coin pushed between his teeth, ready to pay the fare of Charon, the ferryman. People reminded him of his great victories, but he said that any commander who was lucky could win victories. He thought of the funeral. 'Listen,' he said, 'this is much more important. I have never caused an Athenian to wear mourning.'

An Athenian mother, had any been present, might have cried out indignantly at this, and thought of the sons for whom she had put on mourning—one perhaps fallen at the siege of Potidaea in the far north-east, another killed in the great naval battles of the Corinthian Gulf, a third dead of the plague. What right, she might have asked, had Pericles to say that no Athenian ever wore mourning because of him? She alone had worn it three times and there were hundreds like her.

Yet, Pericles was entitled to say what he did. He meant that other men in a position as powerful as his might have used it to get rid of their personal enemies. He had not waged private feuds; he had not even fought for his friends, as Pheidias had learned to his cost. He had fought and thought and built only for Athens, and he had been able to do this because he knew how to handle the Athenian Assembly. He did not need to flatter them; he could afford to be frank. When they showed signs of wanting to go too far he brought them to their senses; when they panicked he put heart into them again; in short, he led them instead of being led by them.

Theoretically, as has been said, Athens was a democracy; but in fact, while Pericles lived, she was ruled by her first citizen. When Pericles died, things were different. The Assembly showed that without his leadership it could become as cruel and as foolhardy as any tyrant or dictator.

CLEON THE TANNER

Cruelty showed itself only two years after Pericles was dead. In 428, after the usual spring invasion by the Spartans, and before the Olympic games, which were being held as usual, Lesbos had revolted. The Spartans had promised to help the Lesbians and in the following year their fleet at last arrived—a week too late. Mytilene, the capital of the island had already surrendered to the Athenians.

The Athenian Assembly now had the people of Mitylene at their mercy. They voted that every man should be put to death and the women and children enslaved. A trireme was sent off to carry out this order. Next day the Assembly came to their senses and sent out a second trireme to countermand the instructions for massacre. It was only just in time.

The person responsible for persuading the Assembly to take their first, disgraceful decision was Cleon, a tanner. The Athenian democracy had reached the point where what is now called "the common man" could obtain supreme power. The politicians, instead of being land-owners, were people who made things and people who bought and sold things.

The 40,000 citizens of Athens, among whom small craftsmen and traders were the majority, had so far been content to enjoy their privileges (e.g. payment for jury service, payment for sitting on the Council of 500) while allowing an aristocrat, Pericles, to lead them. Now they wanted positions of power as well as privileges; and they got them. But they had to struggle among themselves first. Dozens, hundreds perhaps, would have liked to exchange the petty power over a few slaves and apprentices, which they enjoyed in their workshops, for the position of one of the generals of the Athenian people. It was useless for them to try and reach that position by being dignified, like Pericles. The Assembly expected a rich land-owner to be dignified; but if a tanner had tried that approach they would have thought he was putting on airs. The only way for a tanner to win the Assembly's confidence was for him to shout

Young men riding in the Panathenaic procession, as shown on the Elgin marbles (p. 41).
They were army recruits, who wore their hair short. Greeks rode without stirrups.

much louder than anyone else, and to shout the sort of speeches which the Assembly would like to hear—to be led by them, that is to say, instead of leading them (a reversal of the policy of Pericles). Thus, like a cheap newspaper struggling for high circulation figures, Cleon pushed his way to the front.

Nevertheless, by a combination of pushfulness and good luck, Cleon managed to provide Athens with a sight which, at that time, was more heartening than her marble temples, more moving than the work of her tragedians and good for a louder, more contemptuous laugh than anything Aristophanes the writer of comedies could put on the stage. Cleon marched three hundred Spartan prisoners through the town (425).

These men had been blockaded by the Athenian fleet on the island of Sphacteria, in the western Peloponnese. They were

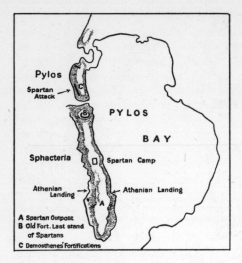

Pylos and Sphacteria

Not everyone approved of this policy. The country people, whose farms were being devastated every year by the invading Spartans, were ready for peace. So was Aristophanes. In 424 he won first prize with the *Knights*, a comedy in which he himself played the part of Cleon. So savagely satirical were the lines he had written for this character that no one dared make him a mask to wear. So he smeared his face with red juice and went on the stage without a mask. Cleon for all his power, could not retaliate.

In the following year (423) Cleon went campaigning against the Spartan Brasidas in Thrace, but luck deserted him. He had served as a general, but never in a lower rank, so he was bound to blunder sooner or later. He gave a wrong order, which exposed his men to the enemy, and was killed as he tried to escape from the rout. His wounds were not in front.

Two years later (421) peace was made. Prisoners and certain conquests were returned. There had been ten years of war and the turbulent Cleon was dead. Aristophanes wrote a comedy called the *Peace*, which looked forward to happier times. In fact there were depths of viciousness and folly which the Athenians had not yet explored.

SOCRATES

The strange thing is that, throughout these first ten years of the Peloponnesian War and the worse ones which were to follow, one of the wisest and most lovable men who has ever lived was a citizen of Athens and saw service in her armies. But though Aristophanes guyed him in a comedy called the *Clouds*, Thucydides

now haggard and in rags but at the beginning of the operation they had been a noble company of Spartan soldiers. The Spartans valued them highly. They could never afford losses which might make them too weak in numbers to resist an attack from the watchful, bitter Helots. They sent ambassadors to ask for peace terms. But Cleon and the Assembly did not want peace. Athens was prosperous. Craftsmen and traders were doing well. They wanted to keep the Empire which they already had in the Aegean and then to supplant the power of Corinth in the west. Peace with Sparta meant peace with Corinth. They were against it. So Cleon would not let his Spartan captives go, and in order to pay for the continuation of the war, he persuaded the Assembly to double or in some cases treble the tribute paid by the "allies" of Athens.

Socrates

does not mention his name. He was not then thought to exercise an important influence upon the state's affairs. Later, as will be seen, he was thought to exercise far too much.

This man was Socrates, born in 468. His mother was a midwife, his father a stonemason, and Socrates probably began life as a worker in marble or stone. There was a group of sculpture on the Acropolis which was said to be his work. But he soon gave up his trade and devoted himself to philosophy.

The word "philosophy", which is made up of two Greek words meaning "love of wisdom", covered the whole of knowledge in those days. "Philosophers" included people we would call scientists or mathematicians (e.g. Thales and Pythagoras p. 26). Socrates was not one of those, nor was he one of the *sophists*, people who made money by giving lessons in debating. His method was informal conversation, unpaid. He would get people talking in a *gymnasium* (open-air athletics centre) or in a workshop or in the *agora* (city centre and market), and by quiet, innocent-sounding questions would get them to reveal what they knew, or, more often, what they did not know.

Pompous, arrogant people did not like this, but it was an excellent method, directed towards an excellent aim—self-knowledge. Socrates was not a crammer; he wanted to develop and bring to light whatever people already had within them. That was why he said he was a midwife, like his mother, except that he was a midwife of the mind—of men's minds, of course. Women's minds were only thought fit for tittle-tattle, on the whole.

Socrates was short, ugly and brave. He served as a hoplite in the Peloponnesian war and on one occasion saved the life of a rich and handsome young recruit. It was the proper thing to do of course, but one's admiration is tinged with regret, for the recruit whom Socrates rescued was Alcibiades. The time was now approaching when many Athenians would curse that name.

ALCIBIADES

Alcibiades was the nephew of Pericles. As well as being rich and handsome, he was amusing, clever, insolent and unreliable. He was about twenty when Socrates saved his life at Potidaea in the first year of the Peloponnesian War (432). He fought in other battles and also found time to lead a gay life in Athens, to talk to Socrates and to race chariots in the Olympic Games. But it was not till after the death of Cleon that he became a leading politician and general.

It may seem surprising that the place of a tanner should have been taken by an aristocrat, but the Athenian Assembly had never been opposed to rich men.

Rich men financed the plays at the great festivals and paid for the maintenance of ships. The Assembly did not dispute their right to be rich, nor did it try to divide up their estates.

What the citizens wanted was that Athens should be powerful and wealthy, so that there should be plenty of markets for their goods and plenty of paid service on juries and on the Council. Alcibiades said he could show them how to keep Athens powerful and make her wealthy again after the huge expenditure of the first ten years of war. So they gave him their votes and did not grudge him his wealth.

The peace made in 421 was called after Nicias, who was now the most powerful rival of Alcibiades. He too was a rich man. He was one of those who rented state-owned silver mines at Laurium and worked them by slave labour at a profit. He was not ambitious—hence his championing of the peace; but neither he nor Athens was destined to be at peace for long.

In spite of the treaty, Athenian troops fought in the Peloponnese in 418, when they supported the Argives at Mantinea against the Spartans, who won. But the bloodiest action of this so-called peace period was not a battle. It was a massacre.

The Aegean island of Melos had never yet paid tribute to Athens. The Athenians, were not much interested in the rights and wrongs of the business. They wanted the money, so they sent an expedition to Melos, forced the islanders to surrender, killed all the men, sold the women and children as slaves and settled a cleruchy (p. 40) there.

One of these women of Melos was acquired by Alcibiades, who had helped to sway the Assembly in favour of the massacre. His next proposal, which the

54

Assembly passed with acclamation, was for the Athenians to send an expedition to Sicily. This measure also resulted in a massacre, but not one which the insatiable citizens of Athens had planned. They did not realise that this time it was their own throats which they were cutting.

SICILY

Greeks had first settled round the coasts of Sicily during the colonising period (p. 10) and in 480 they had united to defeat a Carthaginian attempt to oust them (p. 32). Their unity, however, like that of the mainland Greeks against the Persians, did not last long, and already in 427 the town of Leontini had asked for help from Athens against the Corinthian colony of Syracuse.

Now, in 416, another enemy of Syracuse, Segesta, appealed to Athens. The Athenians sent ambassadors to Segesta. These ambassadors were impressed by the wealth of the place, which the Segestans exaggerated by sending round the same set of gold and silver plate to each house at which the ambassadors were entertained.

Alcibiades looked at it this way. With the massacre of Melos the last resistance in the Aegean had been disposed of. If Athens was to go on extending her maritime Empire she must look westwards. No matter if the Segestans had to be accepted as allies on an equal footing until Syracuse was conquered. None knew better than the Athenians the steps by which an ally might be changed into a subject.

There was also the point that the sympathies of Syracuse, since she was a Corinthian colony, inclined towards the

The famous Venus of Milo (i.e. Melos), dating from the 2nd century B.C. (i.e. long after the massacre). The Greeks are the first sculptors known to us who produced statues of naked people.

55

Sicily, to illustrate the Athenian Expedition

doors of many Athenian homes. If the culprits were agents in the pay of Syracuse or Corinth, as seems possible, they earned their money well, for the outrage shocked Athens. His enemies said that Alcibiades was to blame. After discussion he was allowed to sail with the fleet but, once he was gone, feeling against him hardened and he was recalled to stand his trial. This he preferred not to do. He fled to Sparta.

The Athenians confiscated his property. A list of his furniture, which was drawn up for the auction, survives (it was inscribed

Spartan alliance to which Corinth belonged. If therefore Syracuse should decide to join in the quarrel which, in spite of the Peace of Nicias, still divided mainland Greece, she would join the enemies of Athens. Far better, then, to strike at her first.

Nicias believed neither in the possibility of a new Athenian Empire in the west, nor in the risk of Syracuse allying herself with Sparta; but the Assembly preferred the arguments of Alcibiades, aged 35, to those of the elderly, timid, superstitious and sick Nicias. So they voted to send a great expedition against Syracuse (in the end it amounted to 140 ships), but they insisted that Nicias as well as Alcibiades should be one of the commanders.

When enthusiasm had reached its height and the expedition was almost ready, an extraordinary thing happened. There was a fuss about religion—not about wealth or power, both of which the Athenians took very seriously, but about religion. During the night some people, whose identity remains undiscovered, knocked down or disfigured the busts of Hermes which stood on pillars by the

A 'Hermes'

56

on stone)—12 beds, 4 tables, an embroidered curtain, some chests, a pillow and so on. It is not very impressive. The list has been cited as evidence of how simple were the furnishings even of a rich Athenian's house. Anyway, the state was the richer by whatever these things fetched. The Spartans on the other hand had Alcibiades himself. He said, "Send a Spartan general to Syracuse". That advice was worth many houses full of furniture, and the Spartans took it.

It was in the autumn of 414 that Gylippus the Spartan slipped into Syracuse with 3000 men and immediately put the Athenians, who were besieging the city, on the defensive. During the winter and spring he built a fleet and drove the Athenians from their position, which commanded the entrance to the harbour. In the summer Athenian reinforcements arrived and tried a night attack upon the heights above the city, but they were utterly defeated. The only hope now left for the Athenians was to sail away while they still had the chance. Demosthenes, the general who had come out with the reinforcements, had with some difficulty persuaded Nicias to agree to this, and all arrangements were made when, on the night of August 27th, an eclipse of the moon took place. Soothsayers, in whom Nicias placed great faith, insisted that this was an omen, indicating that departure should be postponed. And postponed it was—for ever.

. The Syracusans blocked the entrance to their great harbour and routed the Athenian ships which were trapped inside. Nicias and Demosthenes then abandoned the ships, the wounded and the sick and attempted to retreat by land.

But the Syracusans were ready for them. The two generals and their army were killed or taken prisoner to a man (413).

"WHY CALL I ON THE GODS?"

In the year when the expedition sailed to Sicily (415) Euripides put on a play, the *Trojan Women*, in which the wives of the defeated heroes of Troy were shown in the first bitterness of enslavement. When he wrote, Euripides was burning with the shame of the massacre of Melos; but now to those among the parched and ragged remnant of the Athenian expedition to Sicily who remembered his words they must have seemed like prophecy. As they shuffled towards the slave market or the stone quarries these once proud citizens of Athens might well recall the despairing cry which Euripides had put into the mouth of Hecuba, Queen of Troy:

God! O God of Mercy! . . . Nay:
Why call I on the Gods? They know, they
     know,
My prayers, and would not hear them
     long ago.*

Athens had suffered the most crushing defeat in her history; and she never recovered. The year 413 was the evening of the great day which had dawned at Marathon, seventy-seven years before. Make no mistake about it, despite all their cruelties and follies those years *were* great. No one reads with exultation about the failure of the Athenian expedition. It is tragic, in the most serious sense of the word. For the "tragedies" which Athenian dramatists gave to the world were plays which moved the audience to pity and terror over the inscrutable workings

*Gilbert Murray's translation.

57

of fate. They were no melodramas in which good enjoyed a simple triumph over evil. No character in them was quite right or quite wrong, and none was petty. Tragedy meant that what was great and noble somehow tumbled into the dust. Aeschylus, Sophocles, Euripides and many other writers had known how to write it. But in the end, as we have seen, the Athenians learned all too well from these incomparable masters and enacted the supreme tragedy of the century themselves.

The Syracusans had a taste for Greek tragedy, too. It is said that certain enslaved Athenians were freed if they could recite passages from Euripides. What did they choose? The disillusioned anguish of Hecuba? (See p. 57.) Or the humble submission to mysterious fate with which many of the plays came to an end?

There be many shapes of mystery
And many things God brings to be
Past hope or fear.
And the end men looked for cometh
    not,
And a path is there where no man
    thought.
So hath it fallen here.*

They must have spoken their lines with feeling.

DECELEA, A THORN IN THE FLESH
The first piece of good advice which Alcibiades gave the Spartans was to send Gylippus to Syracuse. The second was this: "Restart the war; but don't just invade Attica for a few weeks of the year. Fortify a position on Attic soil and hold it."

*Gilbert Murray's translation.

The Spartans fortified Decelea near the border of Attica and Boeotia (413). Raids from this post made the growing of crops more difficult than ever and cut the route to Euboea, where the cattle and goats had been sent for safety. An attack on Athens itself had constantly to be guarded against.

The silver mines at Laurium had to be closed and thousands of slaves slipped away to Decelea as deserters. (There may have been more slaves than citizens in Athens and though they were protected by the law and were less badly off than elsewhere in the Ancient World, plenty were ready to leave.)

Decelea was a thorn in the flesh of Attica. The essentials of a thorn in the flesh are that it hurts all the time; then it festers and hurts more and more: finally the sufferer is ready to pay any price to have it taken out.

The sufferings inflicted by the Decelea garrison were only beginning when, late in the year 413, a barber in the Peiraeus welcomed a customer who had just arrived in the port. This customer mentioned the Athenian disaster in Sicily, little knowing that he was first with the news. The Athenians put him in prison for spreading false rumours; but they soon knew he had told the truth, and as the news spread among the subject islands and cities of the Aegean they began to make plans not so much for freedom, which was not a practical proposition, but for a change in allegiance.

Persia was waiting. She still regarded Ionia and the islands as hers and Sparta was delighted to let her have them on condition that the Persian fleet took over the responsibility of fighting Athens at sea. Thus, in spite of the fact that

Athens no longer exacted the tribute, only Samos, of the more important subject states, was persuaded to remain loyal and provided a base for the Athenian fleet during the closing stages of the war.

ATHENS IN DEFEAT

This closing stage was surprisingly long. Alcibiades, having made himself unpopular at Sparta, was allowed once more to take command of the Athenian fleet, which he did with some success. On the home front the Spartans were not in a hurry. For a people of such high military reputation they were astonishingly cautious. Year after year they were content to operate from Decelea. They never tried to capture Athens by assault. In this they were wise. The thorn festering in the flesh would infect the whole body in time.

The Sicilian disaster roused so much distrust in democracy at Athens that it was possible for an *oligarchy* to seize power (411). Oligarchy—"rule by the few" was a form of government which Athens had not experienced since the 6th century, though it was common in many of the Greek states.

In referring to earlier times the word "aristocracy"—"rule by the best", i.e. the old-established wealthy families, is sometimes used, but the form of government described is the same as oligarchy—rule by a small wealthy group. The change of word simply indicates that, as time went on, the old families were not the only wealthy ones.

The oligarchs only stayed in power for a few months. The men of the fleet at Samos threatened to sail against Athens if democracy was not restored. So in the autumn the chief oligarchs fled to Decelea and a limited democracy, which still excluded the poor, was established. Next year (410), again under pressure from the sailors, who were poor and justifiably pleased with themselves after a victory over the Spartan fleet, the full democracy was restored.

There followed five years in which Spartan peace offers were contemptuously rejected, while good conduct of the war was made impossible owing to the reckless spite of the democratic Assembly. They dismissed Alcibiades because of a defeat suffered by one of his subordinates. (He was finally murdered, in Persia, in

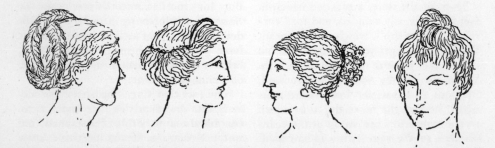

A barber trimmed men's hair and beards, but women produced these styles in their homes

404.) They ordered the execution of six high officers who had helped to win a victory but, it was said, at too great a cost in lives. Socrates, who happened to be chairman on this last occasion, protested in vain. Accusations of treachery were the fashion. A witch hunt was on. No one was safe. Euripides, aged 75, left for Macedonia, where he died in 406. Sophocles, aged 90, had less to fear. He died a few months later and was therefore spared the sight of his city's final abasement.

The end came in 405 when Lysander, the Spartan admiral, after capturing the entire Athenian fleet, proceeded to blockade Athens and cut off her corn supply. The terms offered were that the Long Walls should be broken down and the Empire finally surrendered; only twelve ships might be kept, and Athens was to become a member of the Spartan alliance. She accepted. In a way she was lucky. The Thebans had wanted her totally destroyed. Instead, she was spared to commit one more stupendous folly.

THE DEATH OF SOCRATES

In the year 399 an Athenian court condemned Socrates for opposing the official religion of the state, a practice which in fact he studiously avoided, and for "corrupting the youth", which simply meant that he tried to get young people to think things out instead of yapping slogans. When the penalty was being discussed, Socrates said that, far from being punished, he thought he ought to be given free dinners for life in return for his services to the state. This independent line did not incline the court towards leniency, and they were not interested when Socrates then offered to pay a fine. They condemned him to death.

The method of execution was dignified. Socrates was handed a cup of hemlock. He put it to his lips without trembling. He was not afraid of death, though he did not know what it might have in store for him. True to his often repeated maxim that our only certain knowledge is the knowledge of our own ignorance, he kept an open mind to the end. "Whether life or death is better is known to God, and to God only", he said.

"Thus died the man, who of all with whom we were acquainted was in death the noblest, in life the wisest and most just." Those two quotations are from Plato (the first from the *Apology*, the second from the *Phaedo*).

XENOPHON

The other author who tells us about Socrates is Xenophon. We owe him much. In addition to writing down what he remembered of conversations with Socrates, he wrote a short account of the Peloponnesian War after 411 (Thucydides only completed his history up to that year, although he lived until 400 B.C.). But his most famous work was the *Anabasis* ("March up Country"). This describes how (401 B.C.) he joined a Greek force which had been hired by Cyrus, brother of the Persian King, in the hope of seizing the throne.

The fact that Cyrus had been the ally of Sparta and that this mercenary force contained a large body of Spartans did not worry Xenophon. Cyrus led them and a large Persian army inland from Sardis and after a time made it clear that his object

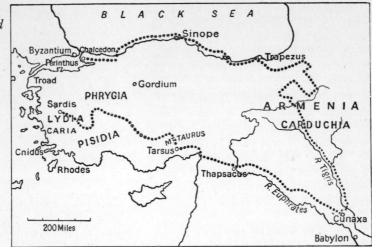

The March of the Ten Thousand

was to seize the throne of his brother, Artaxerxes, King of Persia.

The "Ten Thousand" (we remember the Greek contingent by their numbers) marched through Asia Minor and along the Euphrates to Babylon together with the rest of the rebel army. Outside Babylon there was a battle in which Cyrus was killed. Soon afterwards the Greek generals were murdered and Xenophon found himself in command. He could not move back along the Euphrates, the way they had come, because no supplies were available. So he went north through the highlands of Kurdistan.

After months of great hardship the advance guard's cry: "The sea! the sea!" was passed excitedly down the straggling column and gave the men new hope. They had reached Trapezus (Trebizond), a Greek colony on the Black Sea, whence many were able to return home (399).

However, the story of this remarkable journey cut no ice at Athens, and Xeno-phon was banished for having helped Cyrus, the friend of Sparta.

After that he made his home with the Spartans and sometimes fought for them. He wrote a number of books in addition to the *Anabasis*. Some are not very interesting, but Xenophon's are the earliest *ordinary* Greek books which we have. All the authors mentioned so far in this "Outline"—the poets, the tragedians, the historians—were *extraordinary*. It is pleasant for a change, to have a book about dogs and a book which includes instructions on household management. Xenophon believed in transferring the orderliness of military life to the household which his wife took charge of when at the age of fifteen she married him. Pots, pans, and even boots were to be arranged in neat rows. Everything had its proper place—best clothes, ordinary clothes, weapons, blankets, corn, wine, and equipment for spinning, bread-making or washing.

Xenophon also lectured his wife about make-up. He was against it; he said the way to get colour into your cheeks was to work hard in the house, to mix flour, knead dough, and shake out cloaks and bedding.

The *Anabasis*, though the record of a splendid achievement, is rather heavy going for the reader of to-day; but if, as some think, it was read by Alexander, (p. 63) he may have learned from it lessons about Greek strength and Persian weakness which eventually took him from Macedon to the Indus.

THE FOURTH CENTURY

Twice in Greek history the Spartans appear as heroes—when they fought under Leonidas in the pass of Thermopylae (p. 32) and when they marched under Xenophon from Babylon to the Black Sea. The rest of the time we are continually hearing of their victories but never of their achievements. As the fifth century gives place to the fourth it is still the same story. Sparta has beaten Athens at last. Sparta is supreme, but nothing spectacular happens. She does not succeed in uniting Greece.

In 371, as a result of the battle of Leuctra, Thebes began a brief period of supremacy, which lasted until 362, when her leader Epaminondas was killed.

Unity was as far away as ever in mainland Greece and the Aegean, but in the west Dionysius of Syracuse (b. 430—d. 367—not to be confused with Dionysus, God of Wine) had stopped the advance of the Carthaginians and imposed his will on the Greek cities of Sicily and southern Italy. Most would have preferred disunity to the cruel discipline of Dionysius.

According to one story he arranged a banquet for his courtier Damocles, but had a sword suspended above him by a single horse-hair. This was intended to impress upon Damocles, who had flattered Dionysius, the truth that the happiness of a wealthy and powerful ruler was not unmixed with anxiety. The hair held and the sword did not fall; but Damocles found himself unable to enjoy his dinner. He had learned his lesson.

PLATO

Dionysius enjoyed culture as well as cruelty. He wrote poems, which were recited at the Olympic Games, and one of many tragedies which he entered in the Athenian competitions took first prize. He invited famous authors and philosophers to his court, among them Plato (429–347), the writer from whose *Dialogues* much of our knowledge of Socrates comes. Plato had been away from Athens since the death of his beloved master and had come to Sicily in the course of travels which had included a visit to Egypt. He soon quarrelled with the tyrant Dionysius and left his court, but he paid two further visits to Syracuse after Dionysius the Younger had succeeded his father (367). By this time Plato had settled in Athens again and his *Academy* had become famous. (The word 'Academy' in English means a school, but its Greek original was more nearly the equivalent of a university.) He had written his greatest work, the *Republic*, which consists of a long discussion on what is the best way to educate a people and govern them. His solution was anything but democratic. He favoured rule by a group of immensely well-educated despots—'philosopher kings'—and it was hoped that Dionysius the Younger might become a practical example. The son, however, proved not to be a better pupil than the father. Plato went back to the Academy, and Syracuse, though now the most glorious city of the Greek world, never became the model of good government which the philosophers had dreamed of.

The problem of how best to educate people and govern them remains with us still. The importance of Plato is that he was the first writer to discuss it thoroughly. The fact that it is easy to pick out from the *Republic* ideas which now sound laughable does not matter; nor does the fact that Plato did not make a success of putting his ideals into practice. The *Republic* is not a book which is only for philosophers, or only for kings. Sooner or later every educated man or woman must read it.

ALEXANDER OF MACEDON

Unity, for a time, and a philosopher king, of a sort, finally came to Greece from Macedon in the north. In the year 356 Alexander was born.

Macedon under King Philip, Alexander's father, was already recognised as a rising power. At Athens the aged teacher of oratory Isocrates (b. 436) hoped that Philip would unite the Greeks in a new crusade against Persia. The orator Demosthenes (not to be confused with the general who died in the Sicilian expedition) was for resisting Philip. He flayed the King of Macedon in a series of orations which have given us the word *philippic* (= a furiously hostile speech, a tirade).

Damocles may have looked like this as the sword hung over him. Greeks reclined instead of sitting at banquets.

Meanwhile Alexander was growing up and needed the best teachers. Plato had died in 347 but his distinguished pupil Aristotle (b. 384), a native of Macedonia, was available and was appointed tutor to the young prince. Thus at the age of sixteen, Alexander was in the enviable position of being in daily contact with one of the most brilliant intellects the world has ever known, of ruling Macedonia while his father was away, and of possessing an incomparable horse, Bucephalus. Two years later (338) he fought by his father's side at Chaeronea, where the assembled states of Greece were beaten and lost their independence. (Demosthenes ran away with the rest of the Athenian contingent. He had done his best. Isocrates committed suicide).

In 336 Philip was murdered, so at the age of twenty Alexander found himself king, and commander of the superb army which his father had created.

Using and improving this army Alexander conquered the Persian Empire.* Three great battles (Granicus 334, Issus 333 and Arbela 331) and the sieges of Tyre and Gaza achieved this (332). Darius III fled. Unlike his ancestor, Darius the Great, he had no need of a slave to whisper reminders about the Greeks into his ear (p. 26). The Greeks were hot on his heels. But they did not catch him. Darius was killed by his own followers. Alexander only found his dead body.

Egypt had not been a hard nut to crack. The Egyptians did not mind exchanging one conqueror for another, and their docility earned them a rich reward.

*Alexander's march is more fully described, with map, in *Early Explorers*, by L. F. Hobley.

Alexander ordered a city and harbour to be built at the western end of the Nile delta (331). Like many others which he founded it was to be named Alexandria. In time it supplanted Athens as the centre of the Greek world.

But long before Alexandria had begun to take shape its founder had hurried on, never to return. He was well received in Babylon (there too the Persians were not loved), burned the palaces of the Persian kings at Persepolis and in the following years pushed north as far as Samarkand and through the Khyber Pass to the Indian sub-continent. He won a battle there over King Porus who had elephants on his side, but when he wanted to press on eastwards his soldiers would not let him. They made him turn back. He seems to have become reconciled to the idea of going no farther east, since it was an expedition south, into Arabia, which he was planning, when he suddenly died, at Babylon, aged 33, from fever contracted after a banquet (323).

ALEXANDRIA AND BYZANTIUM

Because Alexander drank too much on an autumn night in the year 323, or because medical science was not yet far enough advanced to cure the fever which his excesses brought on, another experiment in philosopher kingship, or at least in philosopher-guided kingship, ended prematurely. Not that Aristotle had accompanied Alexander, but they had corresponded, and if Alexander had thought of settling down and concentrating on administration, Aristotle, who studied the constitutions of 158 Greek states, would have been the man to advise him. On the other hand Alexander also

The Pharos of Alexandria was a lighthouse built in the third century B.C. Nothing of it now remains, but it is thought to have looked like this. It was over 350 ft. high (St. Paul's is 366 ft.). The light was provided by a huge brazier and mirrors were somehow used to increase its brilliance.

corresponded with his mother, Olympias, a vile woman who had probably been concerned in the murder of his father, Philip. Whether her influence or Aristotle's would have prevailed over the years is anybody's guess.

Alexander's empire broke up after his death, but part of it (roughly, the countries west of the Euphrates) remained united by Greek language and customs; they had been "hellenized". Historians therefore called the period after Alexander's death the "Hellenistic Age", and the centre of "Hellenism" was Alexandria. The lighthouse there was among the seven wonders of the ancient world and Alexandrine learning shone as brightly.

The *Elements of Geometry* by Euclid (323–283) was still a textbook in the

19th century; Eratosthenes (276–196) measured the circumference of the earth by a method not very different from that used to-day; dissection was allowed and medical knowledge therefore increased; the Hebrew Old Testament was translated into Greek (tradition attributed the work to seventy scholars, whence its name —the Septuagint) and Alexandria later became a centre of Christian learning.

The term "Hellenistic Age" is a convenient historian's label to cover the period which ends with the conquest of Greece by Rome in 146 B.C. (Having conquered first Italy and then her great rival, Carthage, Rome had become the greatest power in the Mediterranean.) But in fact, as the Roman poet Horace wrote, Greece was in a sense the victor. The works of her writers and artists had

In 1687 the Turks were besieged by the Venetians in the Parthenon, which had been converted into a mosque (the minaret can be seen in the picture). On Sept. 26th a Venetian shell entered a Turkish powder store. Since then the Parthenon has been a ruin.

66

more effect on the simple, rough Romans than the Roman soldiers had on Greece. Educated Romans began to learn Greek as a second language, but Latin was nowhere imposed upon the conquered Greeks.

So what one may call the 'cultural' empire of Alexander survived through Roman times and took on a new life when (A.D. 328) the old Greek colony of Byzantium, was enlarged and renamed Constantinople. It supplanted Alexandria as the centre of a Christian Greek world which survived until the Turks finally conquered it in 1453. Athens fell a few years later (1458).

Nearly four centuries went by before the Greeks had a country of their own again. In 1821 Byron lamented the vanished splendours of the Aegean:

The Isles of Greece, the isles of Greece!
Where burning Sappho loved and sung,
Where grew the arts of war and peace,
Where Delos rose, and Phoebus sprung!
Eternal summer gilds them yet,
But all, except their sun, is set.

Athens was then an untidy village, sprawling below the ruins of the Parthenon. But by 1832 the Greek War of Independence had been fought and won, and the Turks were gone. Athens began to revive—this time as the capital of a kingdom.

Watch this Kingdom of the Hellenes. The Greeks have given us so much in the past—plays which are still acted, books which are still read, temples and statues on which the sun still shines. What else have they in store?

GREEK HISTORY AT A GLANCE

c 3000–1400 Minoan Ages	Crete supreme.
c 1400–1100 Mycenaean Age	Mycenae and other Peloponnesian cities, inhabited by Achaeans, supreme. Sometimes called 'Homeric Age' because Homer, who lived much later, described it.
c 1100–800 Dark Age	Dorian invasion. Greeks move into Ionia. Homer perhaps lived c 900.
800–600 Age of Colonisation	Colonies throughout Mediterranean and Black Sea. 776, First Olympic games. Delphic oracle gains influence. Spartan system established.
600–500 Sixth Century	Sometimes called the 'Age of the Tyrants.' Peisistratus at Athens. Solon and Cleisthenes found Athenian democracy. Philosophers and poets in Ionia and the islands.
500–400 FIFTH CENTURY	DEFEAT OF PERSIANS (490, 480–479) ATHENIAN EMPIRE THE PERICLEAN AGE. FULL DEMOCRACY FOR ATHENIAN CITIZENS. WRITING OF HISTORY, TRAGEDY AND COMEDY. THE PARTHENON. SCULPTURE AND POTTERY. PELOPONNESIAN WAR (431–404). SOCRATES.
400–300 Fourth Century	Death of Socrates. Athens has lost her Empire, but her philosophers, orators and sculptors are famous. Greece submits to Philip of Macedon (338). Conquests of Alexander (332–323).
c 300–146 Hellenistic Age	Alexandria more important than Athens as centre of learning. Greece becomes part of Roman Empire (146).
146 B.C.–328 A.D.	Greece part of Roman Empire.
328–1453	Eastern Roman Empire or Byzantine Empire starting with founding of Constantinople.
1453–1821	Greece under Turkish rule. War of Independence begins (1821).
1832	Greece an independent kingdom.

Cyrus the Great	549–529	(First King of Persia. Conquered Croesus.)
Darius the Great	521–486	("Remember the Athenians".)
Xerxes I	486–465	(Second invasion of Greece.)
Artaxerxes II	405–362	(The "March up Country".)
Darius III	336–330	(Last King of Persia. Defeated by Alexander.)

A SELECT BOOK LIST

By Elizabeth N. Bewick, A.L.A.

History and Antiquities

BREASTED, JAMES HENRY. *Ancient times: a history of the early world*. Ginn. rev. edn., 1944. Illus., maps, book list. An introduction to the study of ancient history and the career of early man.

BURY, J. B. *A history of Greece to the death of Alexander the Great*. Macmillan, 3rd edn., rev. by R. Meiggs, rep. 1956. Illus., maps. A political history, with a chronological table of principal events and full descriptive notes and references.

CARY, M., ed. *History of the Greek and Roman world*. Methuen.
1. Ormerod, H. A. A history of the Greek world from 776 to 479 B.C. (in. prep.)
2. Laistner, M. L. W. A history of the Greek world from 479 to 323 B.C. 2nd. edn., 1951.
3. Cary M. A history of the Greek world from 323 to 146 B.C. 2nd. end., 1951.
A full standard history for the advanced student.

FAWCETT, RAYMOND, ed. *Greece* ("How did they live" series). Gawthorn, 1951. Illus. A brief description of everyday life in Athens in the fifth century B.C., with a sketch map of the city and a plan of a typical family house.

FARRINGTON, BENJAMIN. *Greek science*. Penguin Books, 1948. A survey of scientific thought from Thales to Galen, on which much of modern science is built.

GLOVER, T. R. *The ancient world*. Penguin Books, 1948. The discoveries and achievements of the Greeks and Romans.

KITTO, H. F. D. *The Greeks*. Penguin Books, 1948. An introduction to the study of Ancient Greece, the country and the people, their life and thought, to the time of Alexander the Great.

LIMEBEER, D. E. *The Greeks*. C.U.P., 2nd edn., 1952. An introduction to the political, social and literary history of Greece.

LIVINGSTONE, SIR R. W., ed. *The legacy of Greece: essays by Gilbert Murray and others*. O.U.P., rep. 1947. Illus. Essays on various aspects of Greek civilisation and its relation to the modern world. For the older reader.

LOWES DICKINSON, G. *The Greek View of Life:* Methuen, 1896; 23rd edn. with a preface by E. M. Forster. A general introduction to Greek literature and thought. Advanced.

MASON, CORA. *Socrates, the man who dared to ask*. Bell, 1955. A biography of the Greek philosopher told in story form and based largely on the writings of Plato and Xenophon.

MILLIKEN, E. K. *The Greek people*. Harrap, 1952. Illus., maps. A brief social and political history.

OMAN, SIR C. W. C. *A history of Greece from the earliest times to the death of Alexander the Great*. Longmans, 7th edn., rep. 1955. Illus., maps. A standard political history for the serious student.

70

QUENNELL, M., and C.H.B. *Everyday things in ancient Greece*. Batsford, 2nd edn. rev. by Kathleen Freeman, 1954. Illus., book list. The story of Greek civilisation in three parts: Homeric Greece; Archaic Greece; and Classical Greece; with time charts and some account of modern archaeological discoveries.

ROBINSON, CYRIL E. *A history of Greece*. Methuen, 8th edn., 1951. Illus., maps. A standard school history.

SELTMAN, CHARLES. *A book of Greek coins* ("King Penguin"). Penguin Books, 1952. Illus., book list. *Greek coins* ("Handbooks of archaeology"). Methuen, 2nd edn., 1955. Illus., maps, tables, book list.

STOBART, J. C. *The glory that was Greece: a study of Hellenistic culture and civilisation*. Sidgwick & Jackson, 3rd edn. rev. by F. N. Pryce rep. 1951. Illus., book list. A social history.

TREASE, GEOFFREY. *Crown of violet*. Macmillan, 1952. Illus. The imaginary adventures of a boy in Athens in the time of Socrates and Plato.

WHITE, ANNE TERRY. *Adventures in archaeology: lost worlds*. Harrap, 2nd edn., rep. 1956. Illus., book list. An account of some archaeological discoverers and discoveries, including excavations in Greece.

WISEMAN, GWENDOLINE. *Greece* ("Four-in-hand" series). Laurie, 1952. Something about ancient Greece, the country and the people; with a chapter on modern Greece and a short anthology of Greek poetry and prose in translation.

Mythology

BAKER, GEORGE. *The realms of gold*. U.L.P., 1954. Illus. Greek legends retold, including the stories of the Golden Fleece, the siege of Troy and the wanderings of Odysseus.

GRAVES, ROBERT. *The Greek myths*. Penguin Books, 2 vols., 1955. Maps. A reference book for the general reader, giving the narrative of the legends, their source and explanatory notes on each.

GUERBER, H. A. *The myths of Greece and Rome*. Harrap, 2nd edn., rev. by D. M. Stuart, rep. 1956. Illus., maps. The standard work of reference for the student.

MANTON, JO. *The enchanted ship: and other Greek legends* ("Chameleon Books"). O.U.P., 1950. Illus. Some of the well-known Greek legends simply retold.

SCHWAB, GUSTAV. *Gods and heroes: myths and epics of Ancient Greece*. Routledge and K. Paul, rep. 1950. Illus. Greek legends in narrative form with an alphabetical index.

Literature: Authors

EURIPIDES. *The Trojan women*: translated into English rhyming verse by Gilbert Murray. Allen & Unwin, rep. 1953. Hecuba's speech (see p. 57) occurs in this play.

HERODOTUS. *The Histories*; newly translated by Aubrey de Selincourt. Penguin Books, 1954. *The wonders of Herodotus;* retold by Eleanor Farjeon. Nelson, 1937, O.P.

HOMER. *The Iliad;* translated by E. V. Rieu. Methuen, 1953, and Penguin Books, 1950. *The Odyssey*; translated by E. V. Rieu. Methuen, 1952, and Penguin Books, 1951. *The Odyssey*; retold by B. L. Picard. O.U.P., 1952. Illus.

PLATO. *The Republic*; translated by H. D. Lee. Penguin Books, 1955. *The last days of Socrates*; translated by Hugh Tredennick. Penguin Books, 1954.

PLUTARCH. *Lives of noble Greeks and Romans*. The Dryden translation rev. by A. H. Clough. Dent (Everyman). 3 vols. rep. 1957.

THUCYDIDES. *The Peloponnesian war*; translated by Rex Warner. Penguin Books, 1954. The funeral speech of Pericles occurs in Book II, Chapter 36.

Literature: Works of Reference

FREEMAN, KATHLEEN, ed. *The Greek way: an anthology*. Macdonald, 1947. Translations from verse and prose: a personal selection.

LIVINGSTONE, SIR R. W. *The pageant of Greece*. O.U.P., rep. 1953. Illus., book list. Selections from Greek literature viewed against their historical background.

The Oxford Classical Dictionary, edited by R. Cary, *and others*. O.U.P., 1949. An alphabetical dictionary of Greek and Roman antiquities, biography, literature, mythology, history and geography.

The Oxford Companion to Classical Literature, edited by Sir P. Harvey. O.U.P., 1937. Maps. The historical, political, social and religious background to classical literature.

TODD, JAMES, and JANET MCLEAN. *Voices from the past: a classical anthology for the modern reader*. Phoenix, 1955. Illus., map. A panorama of the entire literature of classical times from 800 B.C. to A.D. 500.

Modern Greece

TREASE, GEOFFREY. *The young traveller in Greece*. Phoenix, 1955. Illus., map. An account of a holiday spent visiting places of historic interest in Greece.

WARNER, REX. *Athens*: 74 pictures in photogravure by Martin Hürlimann. *Eternal Greece*: 90 pictures in photogravure by Martin Hürlimann. Thames & Hudson, 1956, 1953. Illus. Glimpses of the Greece of the past revealed by photographs of the Greece of today.

INDEX

The page numbers refer to text and illustrations alike. The names of Greek plays and books are printed in *italics*. The meaning of words will generally be found at their first entry.

74

75